DIY Marketing for Beginners:

Your Guide to Maximizing your Marketing on a Minimal Budget

By O. Michele Giacomini

DEDICATION

This book is dedicated to my husband who supports my support of others and my sons who have always tolerated the time I spend to help promote, coach and consult others for achieving success, (whether as a classroom teacher, an education administrator, a public relations/marketing consultant, and now a vlog talk show host). They have always seen the bigger picture that it is important to promote others, because we achieve success when we help others succeed.

~

A special thank you to dear friends Deanna of WineTourDrivers.com, Joe of Crisp Catering & Deanna the "Stay at Home Nurse," who always support my endeavors, and who allow me to support and promote them right back, (even when they don't really need it). Their drive for success and constant professionalism is admirable and inspiring, (and I appreciate their courtesy of allowing me to use them as upstanding examples of how to promote and succeed in business).

INTRODUCTION

This book is meant to serve as a guide to help small business owners or startups, in particular, on how to do their own marketing. Many times small businesses start off with a very tight & tiny marketing budget. If that's your case, as well, then you need to understand that the problem with allocating little funding toward your marketing is that you need to promote yourself so people know about you. Let's face it, if people don't know you exist, how are you going to "sell" your product, service, etc.? Right? Right!

But how do you do that when you don't have the funds? This book is going to show you many low to no-cost ways that you can get a head start on marketing your business, organization, project or yourself. I understand that many people will use this book for marketing all sorts of things. Many times it is for a business, sometimes it is for a non-profit, a book, or an event, etc. For ease in conveying the message of marketing throughout this book I will be writing mostly to target small businesses/start-ups; however, all the information, (for the most part), is still applicable even if you are an author, non-profit, etc. (you just need to get into the mindset of being a "business"). Then take in the information and apply it for how it works for you & your situation.

Further down the road, you may find that you will need an actual marketing agency to help promote you and get the word out, but at least you will have an understanding of all the basics. I often share with my clients that by reading this book and taking my on-line course on DIY Marketing for

Beginners, they will at minimum, have a better understanding of what a marketing company is doing for them, which is very valuable knowledge!

As alluded to, this book is intended to help supplement your learning of the concepts taught in my on-line DIY Marketing for Beginners course. (Thus, the reason it is formatted "workshop-style" with full intention of you writing all over inside)! That said, if you haven't taken the on-line course, you will still glean a great deal of information from this book. But to help maximize your learning and support your efforts, I highly recommend that you take my online course as well. Contact us at Dragonfly Ranch Consulting: info.DragonflyRanch@gmail.com for more details on how to take my online marketing course.

Wishing you the very best with your new business, or small business, (or new project, or whatever it is that you are looking to promote). I hope that you are able to get maximum exposure on a minimal budget!

WHO WANTS A FREEBIE???

Check out my 30 favorite marketing tips for tight business budgets!

Go to this link here today:

http://bit.ly/MY30FAV

Lesson ONE
YOU CAN DIY YOUR OWN MARKETING!

Whether you are a new business, (or an established one), a small business, publishing a new book, promoting some kind of project, or you are with a nonprofit organization, you can do your own marketing on a small budget.

This book will help you with a multitude of strategies that you can learn so that you may DIY Market your business, project or what not, anytime and anywhere in the world, (as long as there's internet, of course)! That's because we will spend a large portion of time on digital marketing. (And when it comes to digital marketing there is a lot to learn)!

Please keep in mind that digital marketing is evolving on a daily basis. Some of the techniques that I taught just a couple of years ago have already changed, and in another year or so, may have changed drastically again so be sure to check for future editions of this book to help keep yourself updated along the way. But for now let's get started!

For all intensive purposes, please think of the marketing strategies I will share with you, (for the most part), as publicity strategies for your business. Gaining exposure of your business's existence, if you will. This book will mostly focus on social media marketing; however, there will be some other great no to low cost ways to market that don't necessarily include social media marketing, (or what we call digital marketing).

One of the great things about social media marketing is that it helps you save time and money.

Nobody wants to waste money!
Nobody wants to waste time!

This book is designed to teach you the very basics of digital marketing and low to no-cost marketing for your business or project, and to get you pointed in the right direction.

It is also designed for you to be engaged in your marketing with me as your coach.

Questions/Ideas

NOTES:

Summary/Reflection/Other

At the end of each lesson, you will find suggested homework for "Hands-On" applications of the concepts I am "coaching" you on. I highly recommend that you read each lesson in the book thoroughly first, then spend a week implementing what you are learning for that lesson. This will help keep it from being too overwhelming, as you will implement in chunks, and you will also establish a routine. This is going to be very very important! In theory, this is a 5 week course. So allow yourself to learn in small chunks, then add on each week. Before you know it, you'll have a great routine by then and will be continuing to learn more and more each week.

Since this book correlates with my online course, please note that Lesson 1 will correlate with Class 1, Lesson 2 with Class 2 and so forth.

Questions/Ideas

NOTES:

Summary/Reflection/Other

Lesson ONE, Con't:
THE MAJOR PLAYERS OF
THE SOCIAL MEDIA MARKETING WORLD

In this lesson we are going to cover who the major players are, (at the time of this writing), of the social media world and which ones are right for your business and/or project.

Who are the major players of the social media world?

- Facebook
- Twitter
- Instagram
- LinkedIn
- Pinterest
- Snapchat
- YouTube

You may be asking, aren't there others? The answer is yes, but these are your "major players" at the current time. So we're going to explore a little bit more about these particular social media platforms for how they can help your business, or not.

Did you catch that last point?

Just because there may be a huge social media platform out there, doesn't mean that particular platform is right for you. It's so important to be sure that you are investing your time and funding for marketing with the best possible fit, or fits, with social media. For starters, it's really important to consider the following:

Who is your target audience?

Not sure what a target audience is?
Simply put, a target audience is a particular group at which a film, book, advertising campaign, etc, is aimed to reach.

Is this all you need to know about these social media platforms? No!

Questions/Ideas

NOTES:

Summary/Reflection/Other

You also need to ask yourself the following:

Who is buying or using my products?
Gender?
Age group?
Geographic region?
Sleeper niches?

You're going to want to match your product/service/organization to the appropriate social media platform and just forget the rest, (at least when you're starting out)! Remember time is money!

Check this out: Here's when and why you should consider using the following platforms. As you read through who their current target audience is, you need to be mindful if they are reaching YOUR target audience. If they aren't, don't waste your time while you are a beginner. Wait until you are well adept with your understanding before branching out, because it will take tweaking to reach YOUR market via a platform who doesn't cater to your target audience.

Facebook:
- Facebook has close to 2 billion unique monthly users. That's huge!
- This platform is predominantly used by females, but widely used by males as well
- This platform is one of the best places to reach Millennials and Generation X individuals
- Facebook is used throughout the day by its users
- Users spend about 20 minutes or more on Facebook every single day, for the most part

PLEASE NOTE: Because Facebook reaches the most and the broadest spectrum of people daily, in a wide span of demographic areas, including the opportunity to drill down and target audiences with with all sorts of special interests, we will focus much of our attention in this class on learning social media marketing, utilizing Facebook. (Many of the techniques will transcend).

Questions/Ideas

NOTES:

Summary/Reflection/Other

Twitter:
- Twitter has about 317 million monthly users when last checked
- Twitter is used predominantly by males, particularly in the age range of 18 to 29
- Is still considered the most oversaturated social media platform
- Its users spend an average of 2.7 minutes on its mobile app per day

Instagram:
- Instagram has around 600 million monthly users and growing
- It's highly, highly, highly visual
- Currently, Instagram is predominantly used by females
- 90% of Instagram users are under 35 years of age
- Instagram's followers tend to follow brands (which means they're more apt to be open to your marketing)!

LinkedIn:
- LinkedIn targets predominantly males
- There are around 106 million monthly users for LinkedIn
- It's very business-oriented, and very much suited for the white-collar professionals, for the most part
- Even though LinkedIn has more male users than female users, female users are not that much further behind. So if you are targeting white collar professional females, this could be a good fit for you
- FUN TIDBIT: LinkedIn's highly active users tend to be less likely to use other social network--meaning this could be your only opportunity to reach this demographic

Pinterest:
- Pinterest is widely used by women of all ages, especially from 18-64
- It is known for being very visual
- While there are less men on Pinterest, male followers are beginning to increase
- Currently, there are more referrals by a pin (post) on Pinterest for making purchases on e-commerce, than any other network today

Questions/Ideas

NOTES:

Summary/Reflection/Other

This is huge for those of you involved with e-commerce. Especially when targeting the female audience. (On a personal note, I have to work hard to limit my time spent on Pinterest because I have been known on many occasions to get on Pinterest at 9 p.m. to look up one little thing I need to find, and suddenly it's 3 in the morning and I'm still on it! During the span of all those hours, I have clicked on gazillions of different pins that I wasn't even intending to look at. But, of course, being completely immersed in all the wonderful visuals that come with this particular platform, I can't resist. In short, for me, it's super addicting! And I love it! And the thing is, I am not the only one!!!)

Snapchat:
- This platform targets the youth, (we're talking mostly 18-24year olds)
- It is not only visual, but usually uses video and short bursts of information

I recommend to my clients whose predominant target audience is from ages 18 to 34, to consider finding unique ways to use Snapchat as a way to promote themselves.

YouTube:
- YouTube is extremely visual! It's all about the videos!
- It has about 1 billion monthly users for YouTube
- The users are predominantly male, especially ages 18 to 49
- There are approximately 2 million video views per minute

Videos could be used in YouTube to promote something you are trying to highlight. If that's what you're trying to do, you may increase increase viewership, and potential leads. Most subscribers will view a video for about4 minutes. Is it okay to be a little shorter? A little longer? Sure, but the biggest impact of your marketing message should be clear and make a punch within the first two minutes of the video.

So is this all you need to know? No!

This is just the tip of the iceberg!

Questions/Ideas   NOTES:

Summary/Reflection/Other

In this overall course (using the book and on-line course), you will learn how to do the following:

- How to setup a social media business page
- How to get more likes/ follows
- Social media post components
- How to create a social media marketing strategy routine & build your social media library
- Tracking and measuring results with social media and Analytics
- Other marketing tips on posts and promotions, and other ways to help your business

Ready to get started?

Let's explore more about the Facebook business page.

When it comes to Facebook you have a few different options:

- the personal Facebook page
- the business Facebook page
- an offshoot group off from one of your pages

You will need a personal Facebook page to start, (regardless of using a business Facebook page or a group).

I highly recommend that my clients use a Facebook business page to start, and then if it is conducive to your business, or your project, use a specialized group page of sorts in order to build a tribe of followers. This would be a sub page for your business page and is not necessarily something that everyone needs to use. Because this is a beginner course, we are not going to cover "group pages" in this particular course. We are going to focus on the Facebook business page.

Here's how to get started with building your Facebook business page. (PLEASE NOTE: Facebook does updates on a regular basis so what

Questions/Ideas

NOTES:

Summary/Reflection/Other

you're seeing may vary slightly by the time you are building your Facebook business page):

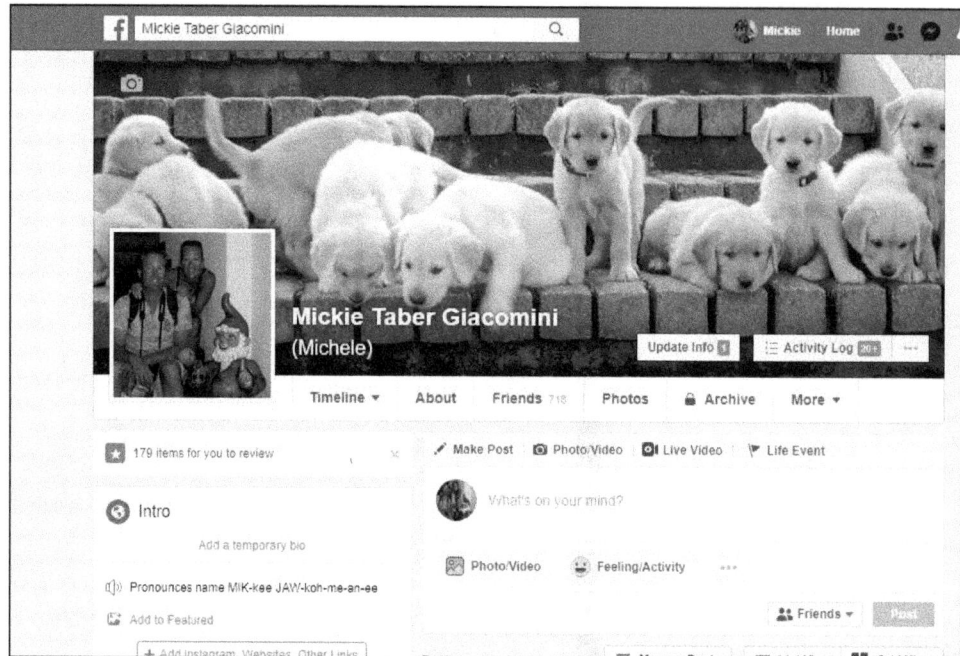

Above is an illustration of my personal page. You need to set-up your personal page in Facebook first, no matter what. **HOWEVER, do NOT use your personal page as your business page! (**If you are already doing that, you will need to stop, immediately, and start using a business page).

Many people think that they can just get away with using their personal page as their business Facebook page, but they are doing themselves a huge disservice if they do this. First of all, the business page is more professional. Secondly, you'll be privy to a lot more features on the business page than you would ever have on the personal page. Plus, you'll be able to use Facebook's low-cost advertising features on your business page. So you need a business page.

After your personal page is set up, you're going to go up to the upper right-hand corner to the drop-down button and open up the window there. as seen in the following illustration. You will need to click on "CREATE PAGE."

Questions/Ideas

NOTES:

Summary/Reflection/Other

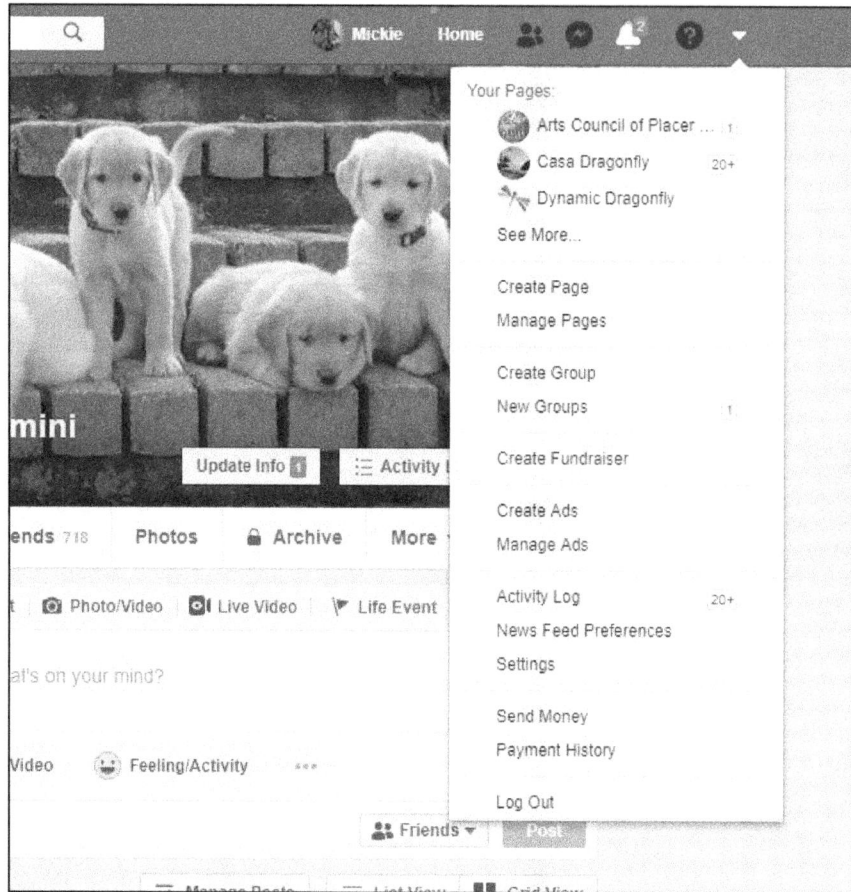

You should get a pop-up similar to this:

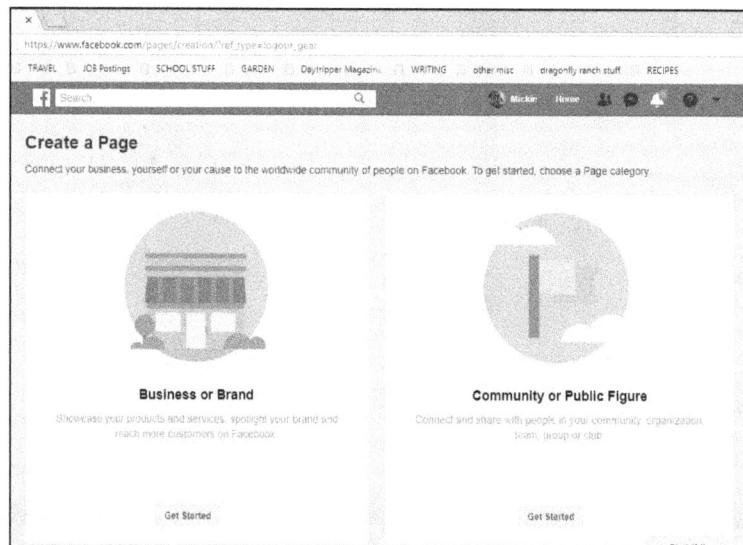

Questions/Ideas

NOTES:

Summary/Reflection/Other

Since most of my clients are usually creating this page for a business or brand we're going to select that side. Just keep in mind that, yes, if you are engaged in something for your community or you're a public figure you would click on the right instead. It would be similar, but different, to customize the page for you & your needs.

Next, Facebook is going to walk you through the whole process. It's really a beautiful thing!

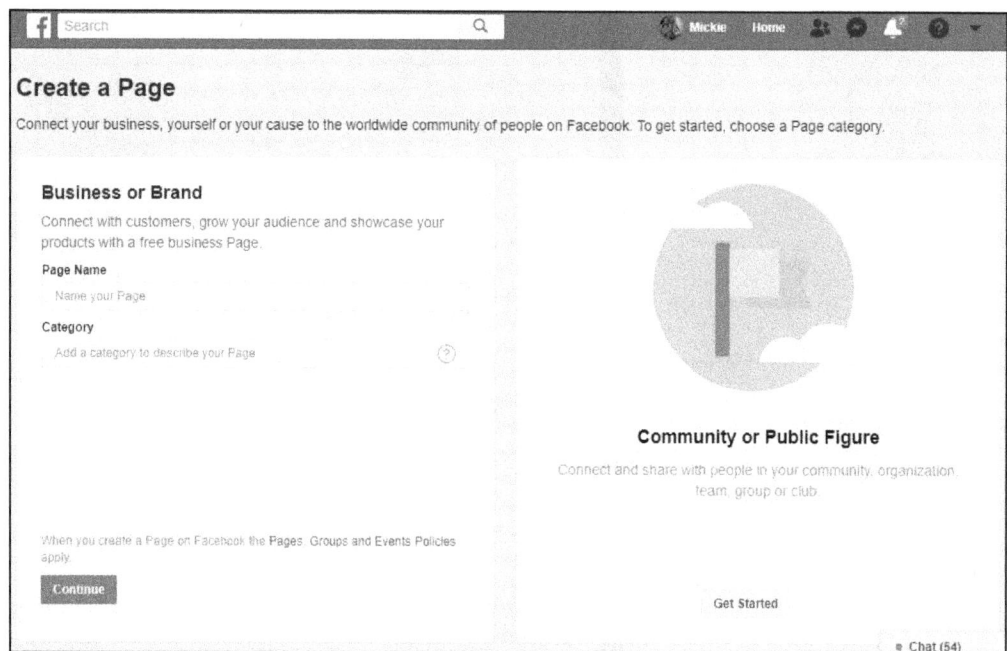

Be sure to include your business name and the category that is most closely suited to what you are setting up a page for, even if it's not exactly the same. Following is a mock business that I am setting up to serve as an example for you.

Questions/Ideas

NOTES:

Summary/Reflection/Other

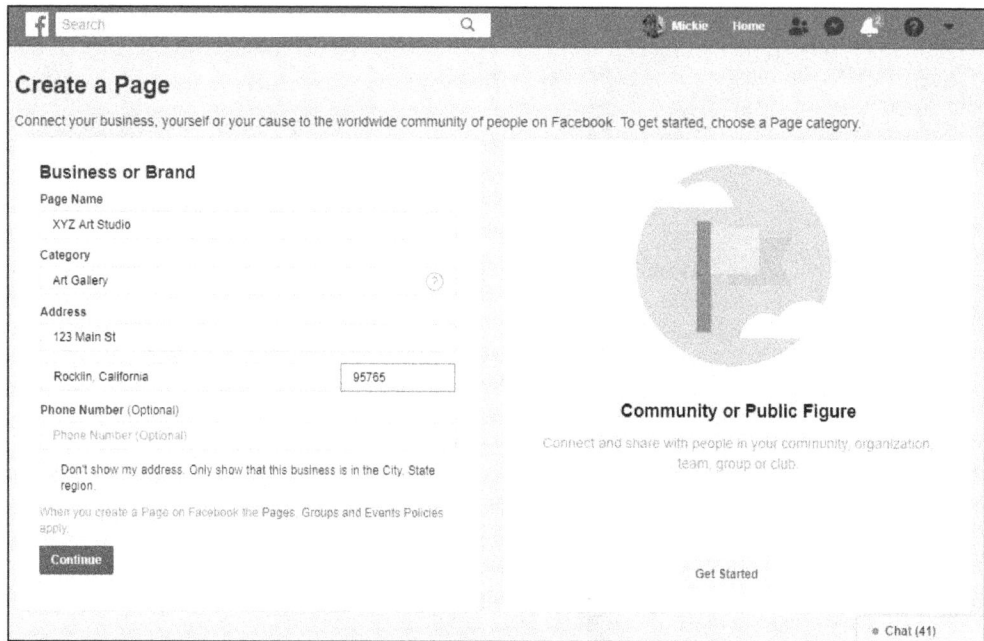

Next, Facebook will continue to walk you through all the different parts of setting up your page. They have really done a great job of getting better and better at helping users do this. Just click on following the tutorial and let the platform walk you through.

No matter what, you need to upload you icon photo and your cover photo. If you don't then you are missing out on the most critical parts of establishing yourself as a professional entity. So don't "lazy out" on this one. It is okay to put something in that relates to your business as a temporary photo, and change it later. But put them in, AND be sure you own the rights to the photos.

Questions/Ideas   NOTES:

Summary/Reflection/Other

Here's what my sample looks like after adding:

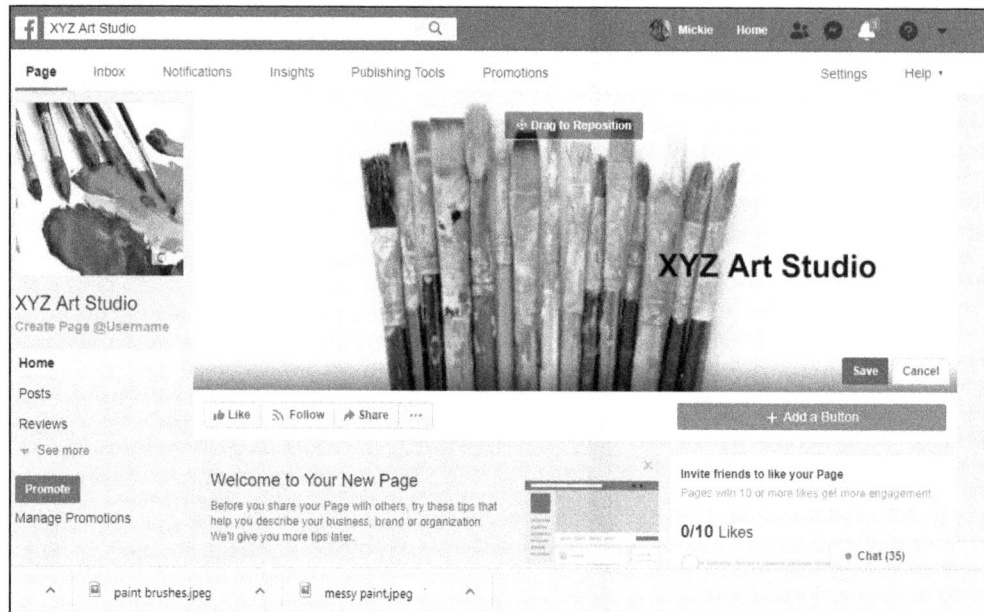

As you can see, it wasn't fancy, but certainly establishes a clear message of what this business is about.

Next, be sure to take advantage of the CALL TO ACTION button. Since it is there, and it is a FREE way to drive traffic directly to you, USE IT! Depending on my client, or if it's for my own business, I always set it up for what I personally need the most. So if it's for a potential new client, I want him/her to contact me, and I want them to contact me by email. So I set up my call to action button to have them be able to send an email directly to me, by setting up my CALL TO ACTION button to send messages to my business email account. Facebook will walk you through this process as well, using just a few steps!

Questions/Ideas

NOTES:

Summary/Reflection/Other

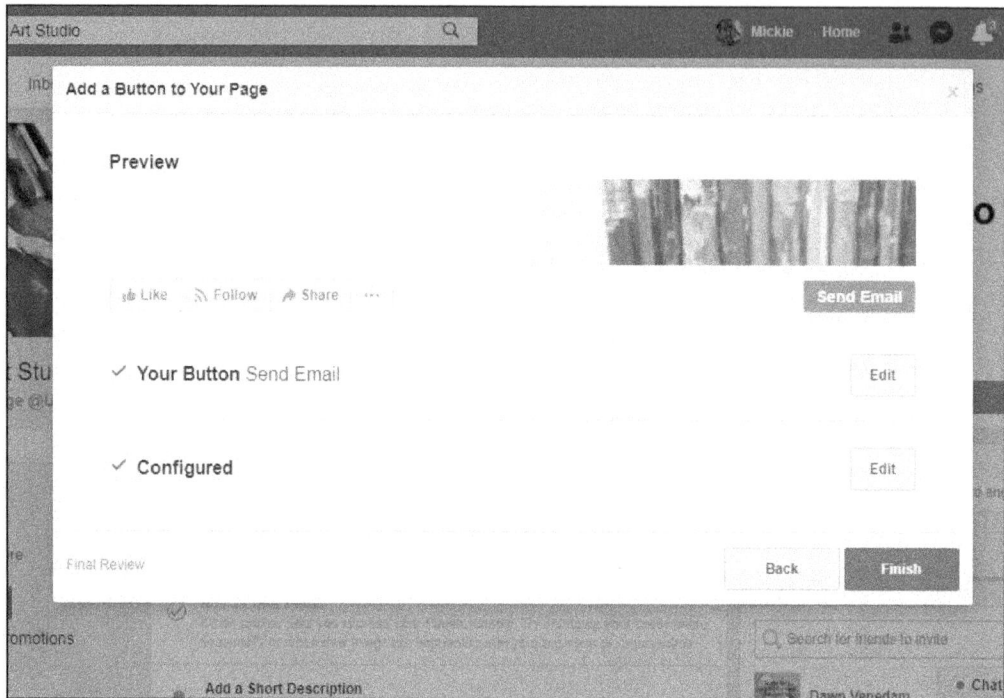

Again, since this platform does such an amazing job of walking people through their set up template, I highly recommend that you take some time right now and pause this book, to set up the rest of your business page. Once you're finished we'll take it from there.

Now it's time to be sure that you put out your first post on your business page! Here's a sample of what I usually do in some variation:

Questions/Ideas

NOTES:

Summary/Reflection/Other

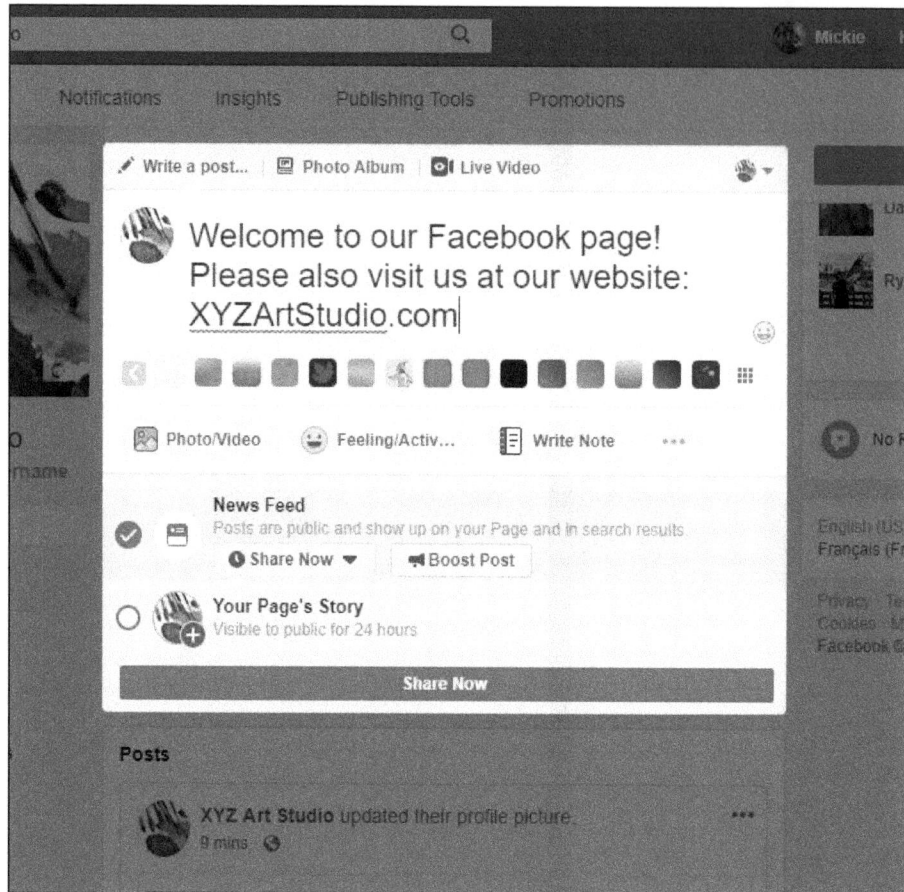

This is the end of Lesson 1. For homework, I recommend the following:

- Spend some time writing out who your Target Audience is for your business
- Reread the part of this lesson going over the various Major Player Platforms, and determine which ones are right for you and your business
- Take the next week to access and explore the other major players social media platform, getting a feel for what they look like, feel like, etc.
- Add your own accounts for the ones that match your business needs and target audience
- Be sure to finish setting up your Facebook Business Page

Questions/Ideas

NOTES:

Summary/Reflection/Other

Lesson TWO

Before we dive into Lesson 2, let's review what we learned in Lesson 1, and add a few new tips!

The Do's and Don'ts of your Facebook business page:

>Do add recognizable high resolution photos for your profile and your engaging cover photo. Even if you are using a temporary, make sure you make every effort to get it switched over to high resolution photos, as soon as possible. Quality goes a long way in this aspect! It's your image on display, and when it comes to marketing, image means everything!

<Don't set up a second professional <u>personal</u> page. and don't use a personal page as your business page! Remember you set up a personal page first and then set up a business page off from your personal page as an offshoot so that you can take advantage of all the wonderful things that come with having a business page (analytics, competitor statistics, advertising opportunities, etc.).

>Do assign roles for your business page; however, don't just add everybody! Only add people who need absolute access and who have extreme buy-in with your business. I do not recommend that you add interns who are not vested in your company. (ONLY add people as admins on your account who care as much as you do about putting out quality information and watching for malicious comments, or recognizing opportunities for a display of good quality customer service).

>Do add a CTA call to action button!!!

<Don't forget to fill out the ABOUT section, and keep it brief, yet descriptive.

>Do add photos and videos to your page. You will have approximately 40 times more of a chance of people being engaged with your post, if you share a post with graphics. (A picture paints 1,000 words--and it grabs attention)!

Questions/Ideas

NOTES:

Summary/Reflection/Other

>Do pin important posts at the top of the page

<Don't forget to decide if you want your fans to message you privately. I recommend that you do! The reason is, is it's always much better to handle a disgruntled customer behind the scenes than in a public forum. That said, if something goes down in the public on your wall in the comments, whenever possible use this to your advantage. (Are you asking, "WHAT????," right now?) What you want to do is demonstrate excellent customer service in the comments. People are watching how you will handle that situation. If it is absolutely derogatory or libel, and you know that you cannot handle this tactfully with extreme customer service in public for all to see, there is (luckily) a delete button! (I do, however, recommend that you take a screenshot first and document any libelous comments, before deleting).

>Do monitor and respond to comments on your page regularly daily if you can!

<Don't forget to promote your page to get more followers!

>Do measure the success of your Facebook effort (analytics)

>Do determine the ideal timing and frequency for your post (we will be discussing more about this shortly, so stay tuned)!

<Don't forget Facebook allows targeting certain audiences with specific update be a gender, relationship or educational status age, location, language, or interest. So zero in when boosting a post (stay tuned this will come up again later)

>And most of all, do unto others as you would like them to do unto you on social media. Karma!

Questions/Ideas

NOTES:

Summary/Reflection/Other

Lesson TWO, Con't:
POSTING UP! WHEN? WHERE? WHY?

Posting on various media platforms differs for the best chance of most reach and exposure. It can be overwhelming at first to get used to.

CHEAT SHEET: (You might consider using as a rule of thumb for starting out, you will also tweak after a month or so when you can begin to get a feel for your analytics)

Facebook-
- When using Facebook it is most effective to keep posts to 100 to 139 characters
- Be sure to utilize graphics, or videos, or links to articles
- Monday through Friday
- Post 1 to 2 times per day
- Most ideal times are 1 p.m. and 3 p.m.

Instagram-
- When using Instagram it is most effective to use 138 to 150 characters
- You must always use photos or graphics (visuals)
- Post 3 times a day
- Luckily with Instagram the ideal time is any time!

Twitter-
- When using Twitter keep your tweets to 100 characters
- Use brief messages with links, graphics and hashtag
- Post 9 to 14 times per day. **NO!** That is not a type-o! With Twitter there are so many tweets going at such a rapid pace, that you need to post frequently in order to try to grab the attention of the followers. Many times your tweets may go unnoticed
- Peak times for posting tweets are between noon and 3 p.m. daily

LinkedIn-
- LinkedIn posts should be kept under 100 characters
- Posts should be informative in nature, and oftentimes you will see that they have links to articles

Questions/Ideas

NOTES:

Summary/Reflection/Other

- Peak time is 8 a.m. Monday through Friday. Secondary peak times are noon and 5 p.m. Monday through Friday

YouTube-
- The average YouTube video posted is 4 minutes 20 seconds
- Usually the first two minutes of a YouTube video are watched at the highest rate
- When using YouTube only post one per day

If this seems like a little much, first of all, you should ONLY be utilizing the platforms that best match reaching your target audience for your business or project, when starting out. For an even more streamlined beginner strategy, use the following **SUPER SIMPLE CHEAT SHEET**: (You will get better as you get more acclimated to your platforms that you're using. Plus, after you're about a month or so in, you can begin reviewing analytics to drive your posting times and frequency)

DAILY POSTS-

Mondays-Instagram for increased likes/follows

Tuesdays-LinkedIn gets most engagement

Wednesdays-Post out on Facebook at your most peak time (1pm for starters)

Thursdays-Facebook and Twitter are a must today!

LATE NIGHT-

SnapChat-Between 10pm & 1am

Pinterest-9pm

Questions/Ideas

NOTES:

Summary/Reflection/Other

IMAGES:
Now that we've covered your beginner cheat sheet(s) on when to post, let's discuss which kinds of post images you should use. As you may have realized, images/graphics are extremely critical for grabbing the attention of your followers, so that your followers will actually pay attention to the message you are trying to convey. Remember, you aren't the only one posting out there. Your followers have many people vying for their attention!

Some of the different sorts of images you can use are as follows:

- Quote graphics (memes)
- Striking color palette
- High-quality stock photography!
- Screenshot
- Infographics
- Personal photos
- Behind the scenes shots of workplace (people just love these!)
- Images that reflect your brand or Essence
- Action shots

Infographics-
Infographics are a great way to display data in a more engaging format, since most people tend to be very visual. By adding photos/images to go along with data you're explaining, you're more apt to elicit engagement.

Personal photo- (behind the scenes workplace photo)
Many people gravitate to photos that show see behind the scenes of what's going on regardless of what the business, show, or event is. Taking a moment to take some candids of your workplace or people getting ready for a big event at your workplace, etc. is a great way to capture the interest of your followers, (they feel like they've got the insider view, and are in the know of what's going on behind the scenes at your business this way).

Photos reflecting your brand or essence-
It is crucial that you select photos which really reflect what you're all about. One of the companies that does a great job on their Facebook page is Voss water. Take a look at their Facebook page and note the different types

Questions/Ideas

NOTES:

Summary/Reflection/Other

of images they are displaying for their followers. It all comes back to the water, and their water! Think about the type of photos you need to be taking in order to convey your business's message and have each photo all relate back to whatever you are truly about.

Action Shots-
When posting photos or even when using them in your marketing materials, consider using action shots. These would be photos that display a movement that helped the viewer see movement in the photo. What this does is help attract the person looking at the photo and draws them in to wanting to learn more about the message you're trying to convey. Here's a couple sample photos to illustrate the feeling of movement:

Note how you can actually see the movement of the legs and the water itself. This helps attract the eye of the viewer and hold their attention long enough to begin to want to know more about the message behind the photo.

POST CURATION: How much and what?
Now you know when to post and more about the types of images you need to add to go along with your posts; but, you also need to learn more about post curation. This means building your social media library so that you can actually recycle some of your posts and use them again in the future. It's important to know about how much and what to be curating as well.

Questions/Ideas | NOTES:

Summary/Reflection/Other

If you're thinking that curating sounds like a museum, well you're not too far off. We're thinking more along the lines of a library, however. So think about how a library curates books for people to check out. You're going to build a social media library of posts for your followers to "check out." This is going to be a bit of work in the beginning, but it's going to save you a lot of time in the long run. (Please note: this is one of the projects I often get tapped to help people with because it can be overwhelming at first. And once I've built a social media library for a client I hand it over to them and then they take it from there. The point is, be prepared for it to be overwhelming at first, but it will be worth it when you're finished, because you will be saving time for future posting).

When deciding on how much to actually curate were talking about different information that you do research and provide for your followers versus how much is your own created content. A good rule of thumb is to bring in about 35% of outside resources for what you post out, and then the other 65% should be your own original stuff that you create yourself.

You need to figure out what or why you need to curate as well.
- Are you curating to entertain or to share valuable information?
- To define your followers personality?
- To establish relationships?
- To feel involved in the world around them like for example self-fulfillment or to spread awareness about brand or causes?

This is a critical piece because you don't want to waste time looking for different resources to help educate your followers or keep them interested in and be all over the place. So stay focused on what your WHY is for your business, curate article, etc. that go along with that "mission." That way you can dive in and seek the most pertinent information to share with your followers. (Just be relieved that you don't have to create it ALL on your own)!

Your followers are going to appreciate if you share a link to a great article that would be of interest to them, which also relates to your business. This helps your followers think of you when they think of that article, and what you might be able to do to help them remedy a maybe similar situation that the article covers. You also might be letting your followers know about an upcoming event that's going on in the community, etc. that they

Questions/Ideas | NOTES:

Summary/Reflection/Other

would be interested in, which also relates to your business. Or perhaps you will be featured at a speaking event, or a trade show, or another community event, and you are helping to not only promote that event but encouraging your followers to stop by and visit you or come see you speak (or whatever the case may be).

WHERE TO FIND YOUR RESOURCES:

It's going to be important that you analyze which of your posts are making the biggest impact, on a regular basis. That's going to help drive your time of seeking sources to share with your followers. Here are some tips to help with finding your sources below.

- Reshare posts (retweet, repost)
- Manual research (industry newsletters, blogs, publications, videos, infographics, quotes)
- Repurpose and curate your own stuff (conduct interviews, etc.)
- Company news, mentions of the company in news articles, etc.
- Promotional content--brand updates, promotional offers, event information, teasers of upcoming products
- Photographs of workshops, training sessions and other such company event
- Work previously done (before/after photos, success stories and happy experiences of customer)
- Your employees' achievements
- Community work done by your company

So now you have all these posts, what next?

For your next step, I highly recommend that you build a social media calendar. You will use your social media library (a collection of your posts) to fill in your calendar.

Some people like to use an actual calendar with notes, I recommend you use an electronic calendar where you can add your post verbiage, notes with links, and to be able to make some side notes on which are the best

Questions/Ideas | NOTES:

Summary/Reflection/Other

post. (And of course, this helps to be able to save much time by copy/pasting in the future)! Think of this as a database (in fact, I use a spreadsheet for mine).

It's really important that once you build your library you rotate every four months on your calendar of posts. At first, you could go ahead and rotate every three months. But, as you build up your library, try really hard not to reuse the same post in less than four months.

Why the redundancy? First of all, hopefully in four months you will have a bunch of new followers who never read the first posts. This is great for them as they will be exposed to the repeated posts for the first time. Also, after four months have gone along, if you post a repeat post, those that saw the original may be grateful that you reposted because they've been looking for that post or they were just recently thinking of it or what not. So it's okay as long as it's not being reposted every other day! Again good rule of thumb is every four months but no sooner than every three months.

SEARCH ENGINE OPTIMIZATION: Do I need to call a mechanic for that?

A SEO (or search engine optimization) is the name given to activity that attempts to improve search engine rankings. If this sounds like a foreign language, here's what I mean:

When you are on the internet and you are wanting to search out something, you type in the subject name (keyword or keywords) of what you are looking for, right? OK, then you get a bunch of listings, hopefully for resources that you can look at to help you find whatever it is you're trying to look for in the first place.

An example of this would be trying to find the vacation rental business called "Casa Dragonfly." If I type in "Casa Dragonfly" into the search bar I should get different results that come up with information on Casa Dragonfly. The results in Google, for example, will display based on what it considers to be relevant and authoritative, when tying in those keywords, "Casa Dragonfly." (Authority is mostly measured by analyzing the number and quality of links from other web pages).

Questions/Ideas

NOTES:

Summary/Reflection/Other

Simply put, your web page has the potential to rank in Google, so long as other web pages link to it. You want your business web page to come up at the very top when somebody is searching for the topics related to them, and especially if they're typing in the name of your business. Here's an example:

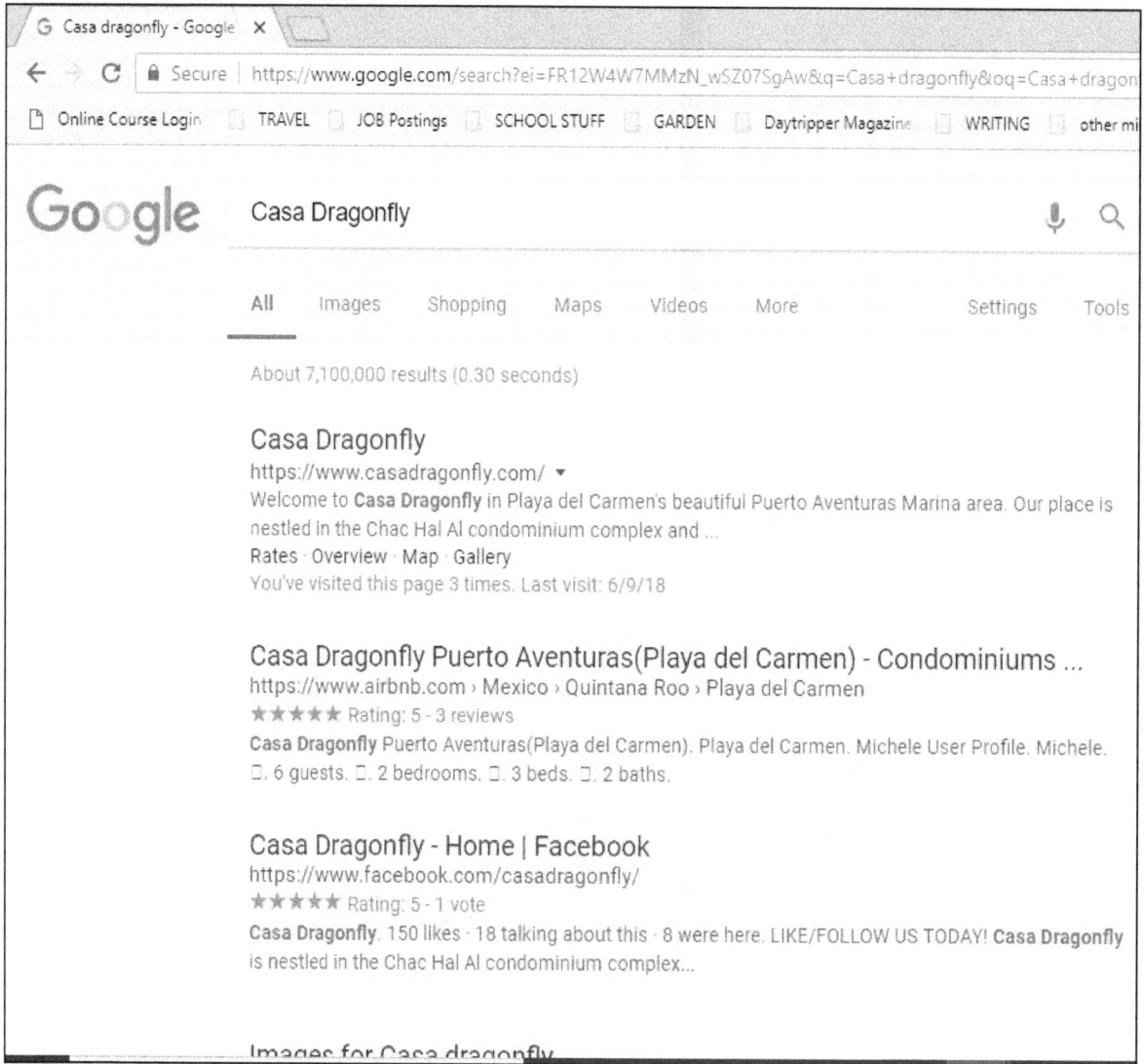

As you'll notice with typing in "Casa Dragonfly" as a vacation rental to get more information, the top listings that Google brings up are all related to the same business. This is a very good thing! At the time of this search above, this business came up as the very top out of over 7 million possibilities. That's what you want your business to do! You want your business to rank at the very top.

Questions/Ideas

NOTES:

Summary/Reflection/Other

It's important for you to realize that this was no happy accident. This took much thought and much work to get this business up to the very top and keep it there. It means constant mindfulness to make sure the name & website address is getting out on the internet through a variety of sources. This means using social media, writing articles that include the business name & website, putting out advertisements with the name of the business & website, and so much more! Especially including the business name & website in your social media posts. Those are just some of the strategies and techniques you need in order to help boost you up in the SEO.

NO TIME TO SIT AROUND POSTING 24/7? No worries! Use a scheduler.

Professional digital markers are not really awake 24/7 making posts for their clients. (However it may sometimes feel like it)! We use schedulers and we buffer our posts so that they will be scheduled to post at certain times, on certain days, in the future. It's still time-consuming but we save time by loading a lot of our posts all at once. It also helps us to be able to engage in smart digital marketing strategies to promote whatever it is that we need to promote over a given time.

The schedulers I like to recommend, at this current time are:
- Buffer (especially for beginners, they are fantastic when you're just starting with scheduling)
- HootSuite
- Facebook's Internal Scheduler

At the time of this writing, my favorite FREE, no push notification, desktop Instagram scheduler is no more.

While I am unable to recommend YET, I am now exploring options with OneUp, Later and Planoly. Again, digital marketing and the programs and apps are constantly changing, so you have to be ready with a backup, in order to make things easier for you. However, there have been some whisperings recently that many schedulers are able to schedule for Instagram without push notifications, for business accounts. So that said, we may now be able to finally bypass the push notification.

Questions/Ideas | NOTES:

Summary/Reflection/Other

What is a push notification?

In its simplest terms, a push notification, (when it comes to Instagram), is an alert for you to do a final "push," or confirmation, on a scheduled post, at the time you need it to post. Some people like this, some people don't, some could care less. It is all about personal preference. Some people are okay with loading all their Instagram posts into a scheduler and then "pushing" when the time comes, while others feel is fruitless since they need to push the post at the time they scheduled anyway. Either way, it is totally up to you to schedule and or not.

BUFFER-
I highly recommended Buffer for beginners for its straightforward simplicity. Plus, Buffer does a great job with some of their videos to help walk you through the process and understand what it is you're doing to schedule and how to do it.

HOOTSUITE-
Once you get the hang of scheduling, I highly recommend trying Hootsuite when you are using two or more social media platforms for posting. I like how well-organized it is, and I love being able to see everything on my dashboard at once.

Questions/Ideas

NOTES:

Summary/Reflection/Other

FACEBOOK INTERNAL SCHEDULER-
One of the wonderful features with Facebook is that they have an internal scheduler. So if, for the beginning, you are only using your Facebook business page, I highly recommend that you stick with the Facebook internal scheduler. It's a great way to keep everything in one spot and be able to view at a moment's notice what you have scheduled for future posts. It's easy to use and is available with just a quick click when you are actually writing your post. Another great thing is that you can use your posts for Facebook and then do what we call a boosted post, which is paid advertisement, in the same vicinity on your page. Here's how that would look on Facebook:

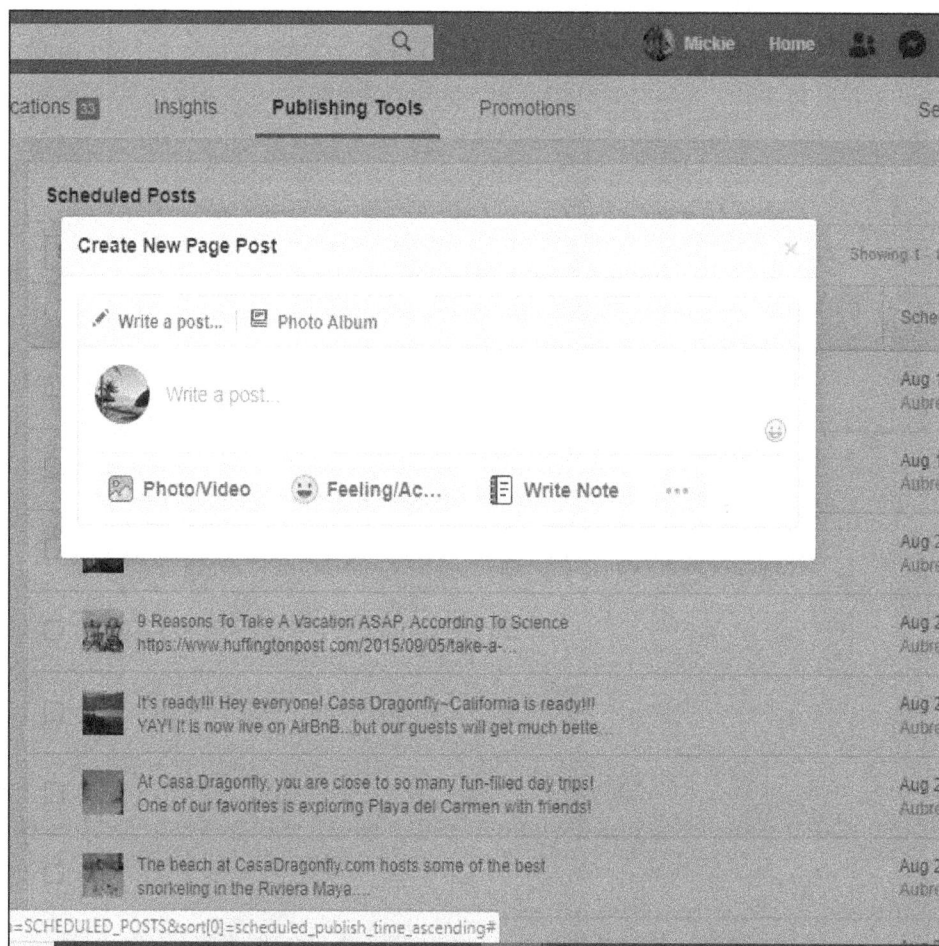

Questions/Ideas

NOTES:

Summary/Reflection/Other

Start off by creating your post.

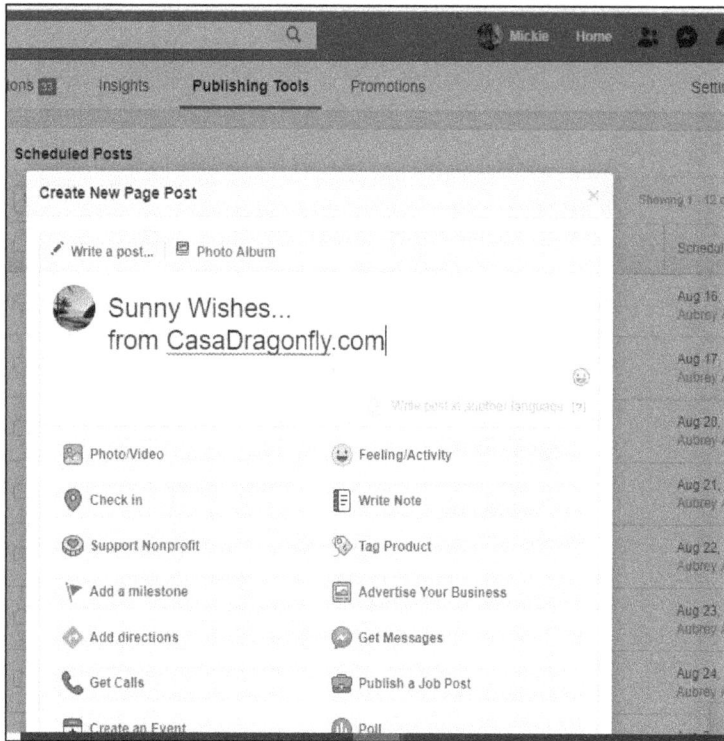

Be sure to add a graphic to capture attention!

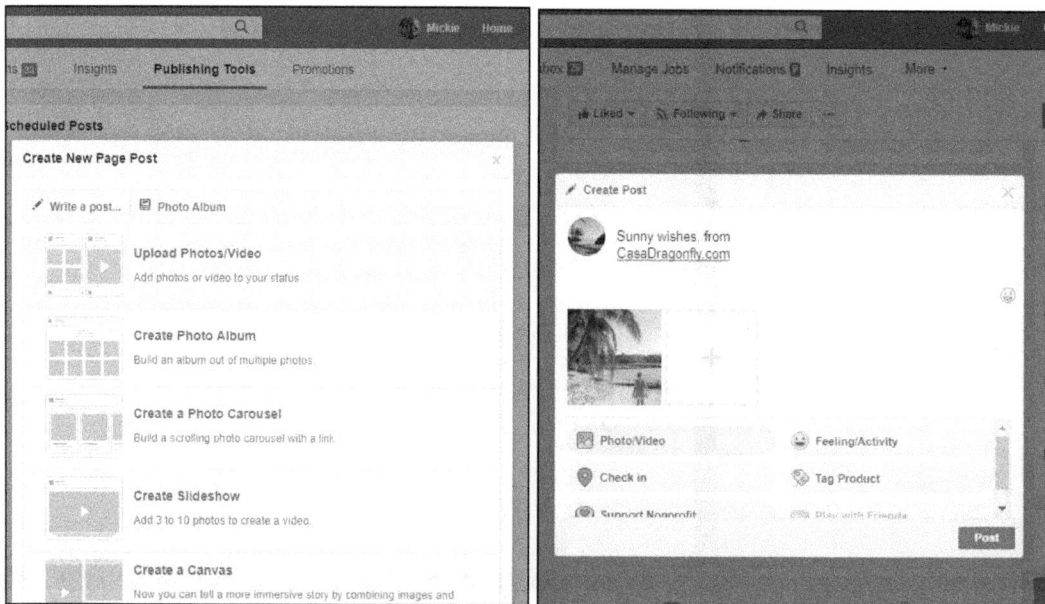

But before you hit submit, DON'T! Instead, click on the drop-down arrow to SCHEDULE.

Questions/Ideas

NOTES:

Summary/Reflection/Other

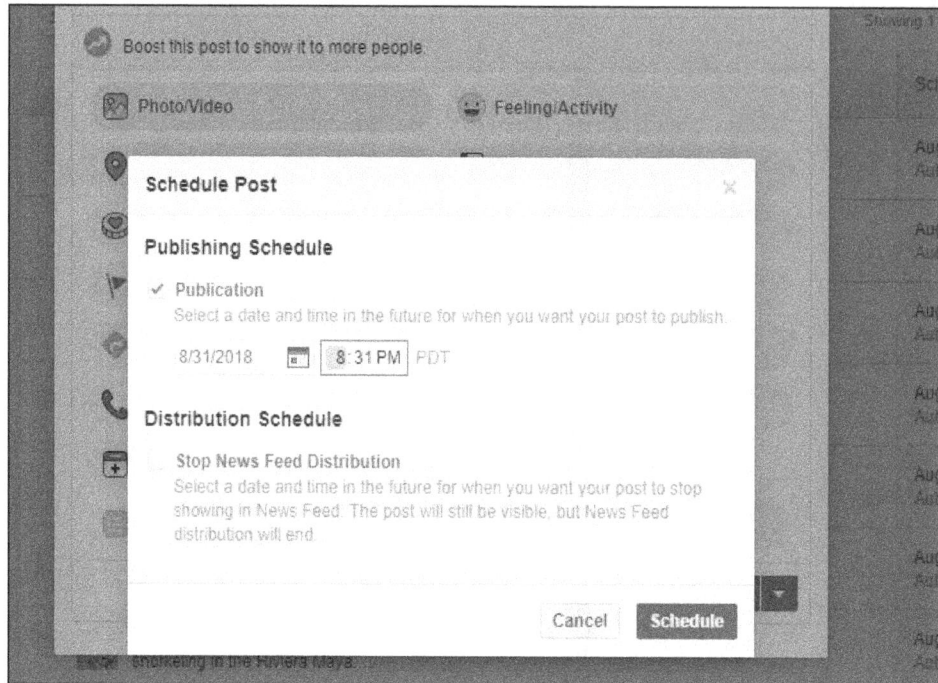

You will need to fill in the date and time you need the post to post out. A great thing is, if you find you need to change this, you can by editing it!

This is the end of the Lesson 2. Over the next week you need to practice the following:

- Write 3 posts for your Facebook Business Page, and practice adding them to the Facebook Internal Scheduler
- Curate 3 photos to use for Facebook (& if you are also using Instagram or other social media, you may be able to use those photos with comments for them as well). JUST BE SURE YOU OBTAIN LEGALLY! No copyright infringement please!
- Curate 2 articles for use on your page and to keep in your Social Media Library.

Questions/Ideas

NOTES:

Summary/Reflection/Other

Lesson THREE:
LINKS, HASHTAGS & KEYWORDS...OH MY!

Now that you have and idea about what post are let's start to take it up a notch. There are some very important aspects of a post. as you well know. We've gone over the basics you need to have and the right amount of characters and images, as well as when to post. But what you also need to incorporate are:

Links
#Hashtags
Keywords

LINKS-
When it comes to Links, we're talking about URL links that will help drive people to the particular area on the internet that you're trying to get them to see. Be sure you're adding the link to your website on your posts, on a regular basis. We want your followers to visit your website, right? So do yourself a favor and send them there!

For example, everything that has to do with my coaching and consulting business, I make sure I add my website address to it.I do this for a couple of reasons. First, it drives the traffic, as mentioned before, to my website. Second, it helps to keep bumping my website up in the SEO rankings.

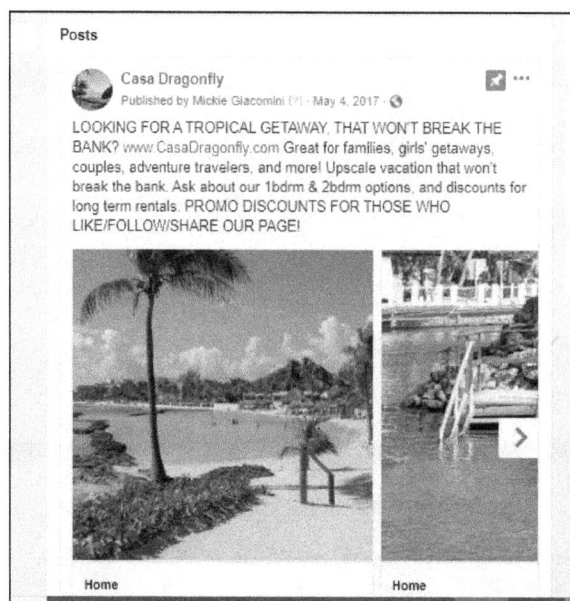

Questions/Ideas

NOTES:

Summary/Reflection/Other

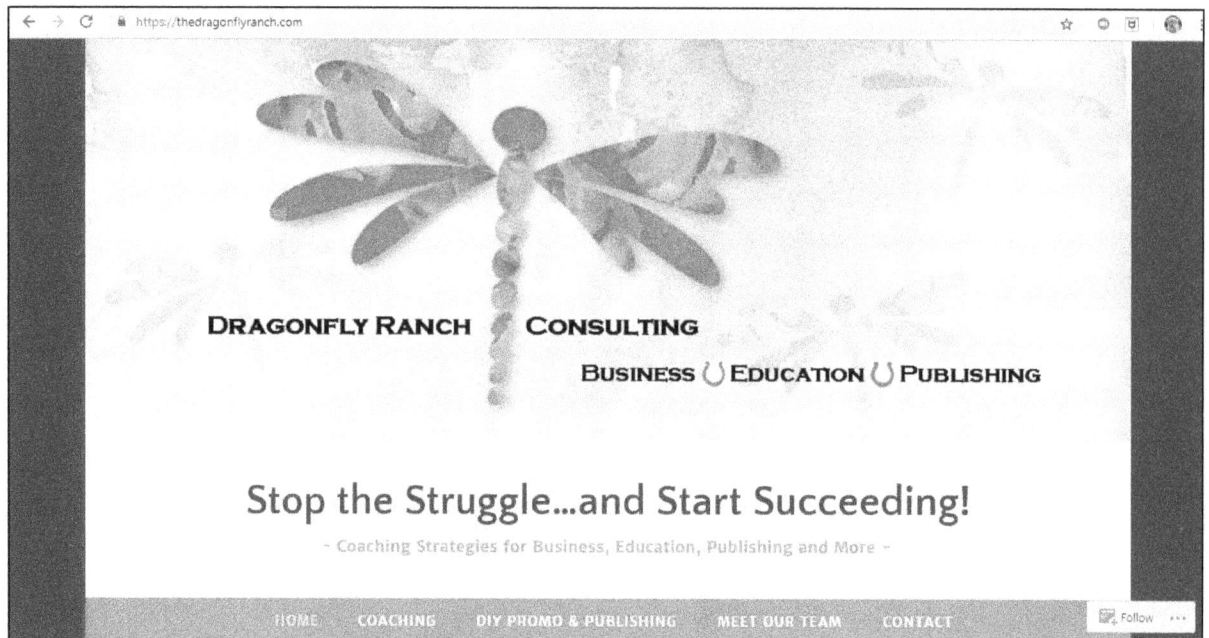

Many times we will type a tease post or a partial post. This would be a post with partial information on it and we offer add the link to the website for more information, or to sign up now, etc., so people will go there to get more information on what is being marketed. This is smart marketing.

Something you will want to double-check is that you add your link to the content you curated. Some people plan to share a great article and forget to add the link, so no one ends up seeing it. YIKES! Make sure that's not you!

I always recommend that you test the links before you have the post to go live. That way you are assured that the link you are sharing is actually going to go where you want it to. There's nothing worse than to make that mistake, and then have tons of people posting about your mistake in your comments that you goofed on the link that you shared.

I also share with all my clients that they need to be sure that their website link is on all of their social media profiles, and vice-versa. Meaning, on their websites they will need to have all their social media profiles listed so people can follow them on whichever platforms they are using.

Questions/Ideas

NOTES:

Summary/Reflection/Other

#HASHTAGS-
What is it? I thought that was the POUND SIGN!

hashtag: *A word or phrase preceded by a hash mark (#), used within a message to identify a keyword or topic of interest and facilitate a search for it. Whenever a user adds a **hashtag** to their post, it's able to be indexed by the **social** network and becomes searchable/discoverable by other users.*

Example:

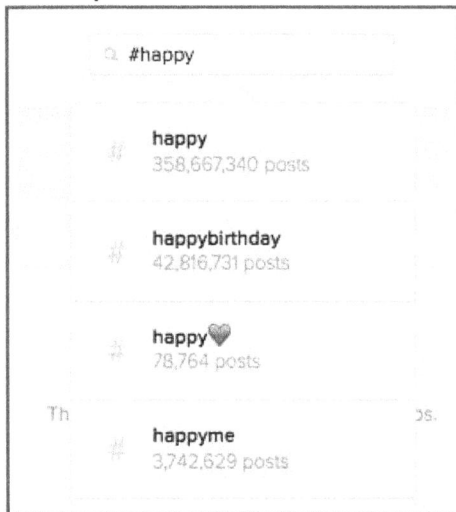

What's the most effective way to use?
BRANDED HASHTAG-Use your business name with a hashtag to help bring in new customers
(Ex: #DragonflyRanch)
This is also a way to be connected to certain content that relates to your business (#marketing #DragonflyRanch) #Oracle #XYZStudio #art #CasaDragonfly #vacation

COMMUNITY HASHTAGS-Pic of the Day, etc
MATCH UP TO THE RIGHT HASHTAG
Instagram gets about 12% more views when using a hashtag

YOU ARE USING FOR DISCOVERABILITY--SO DO A SEARCH FIRST!
Twitter is actually a great resource for seeing which hashtags are most discoverable, but check out my Pro Tip under keywords next, as it is my time saving marketing hack.

Questions/Ideas

NOTES:

Summary/Reflection/Other

KEYWORDS-
Keywords are words we use in our marketing to help drive our ranking up in Search Engines, (like <u>Google</u>).

My Pro Tip is using Wordstream's free keyword tool**:** <u>www.wordstream.com/keywords</u>

It not only helps with ranking, it also helps with discoverability! Let me clarify. You will use these "keywords" to embed in your articles, posts and on your website, to **boost your rankings**. BUT! You can also seek out these same words and hashtag them, to make your posts **more discoverable**. So it serves a couple of purposes.

By looking at keywords and which words are the most discoverable, you'll be able to use in a variety of marketing communications:

- POSTS
- PROMO MATERIALS (ADS)
- ARTICLES
- BLOG POSTS

Following is an example of how I would use Wordstream to find the keywords to use when marketing the XYZ Art Studio:

Questions/Ideas

NOTES:

Summary/Reflection/Other

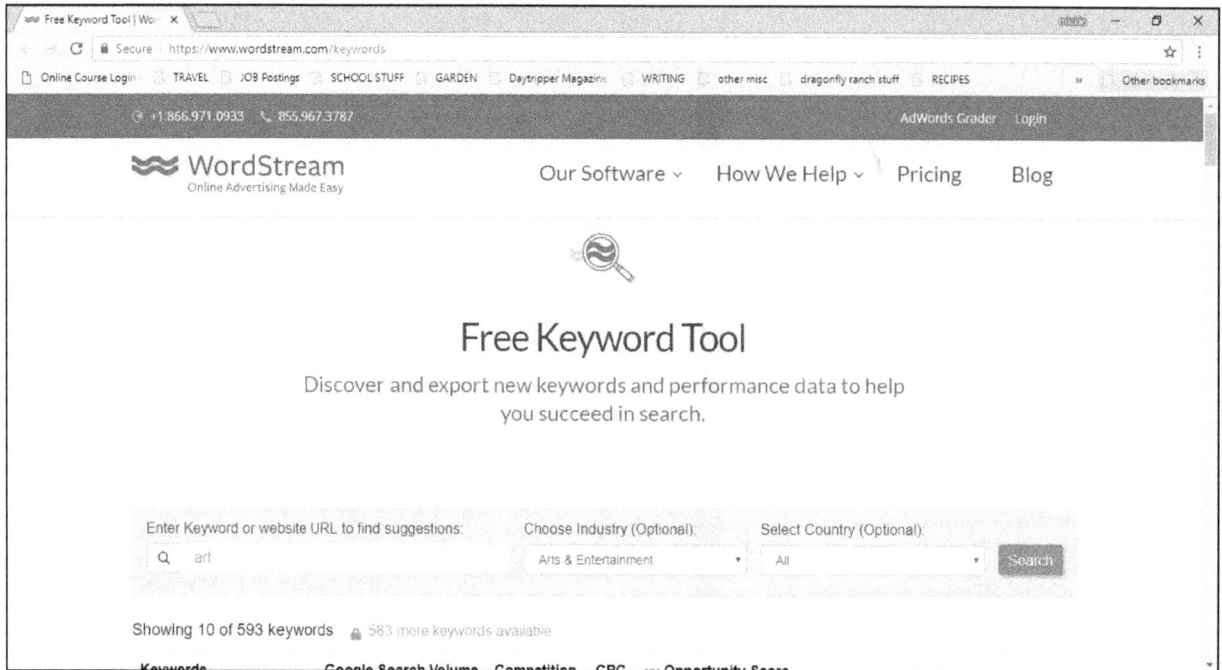

As you can see, I've typed in the word "art" and also added the industry of "arts and entertainment."

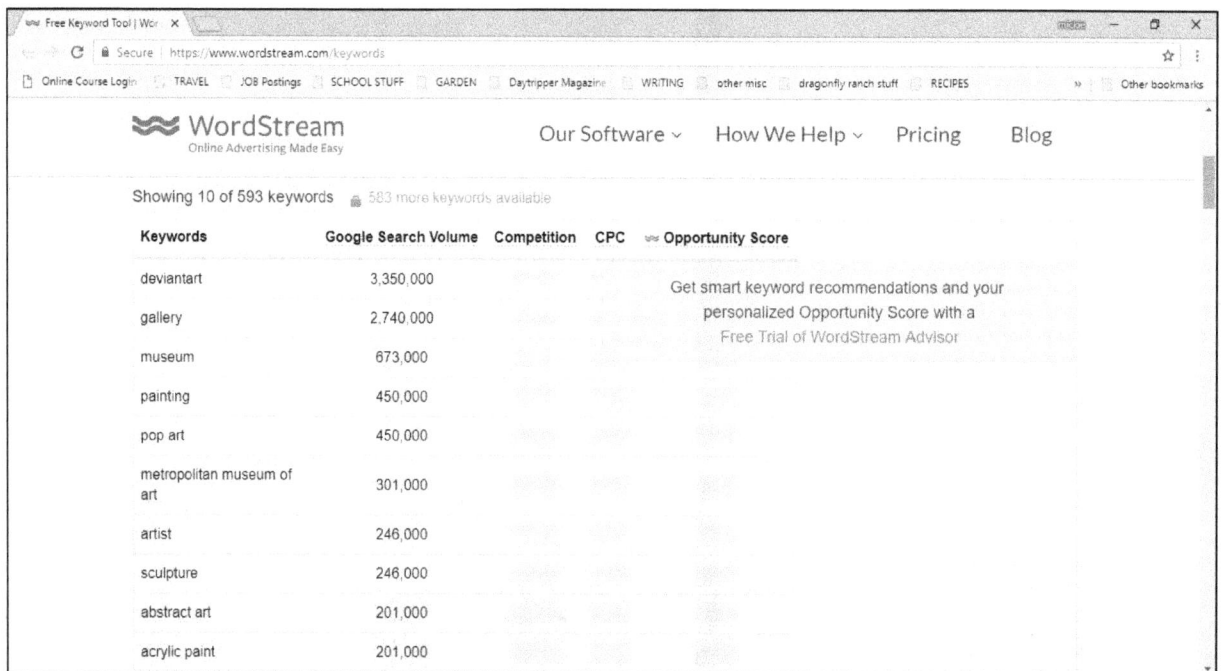

Once I click on that, the most popular, or discoverable, words appear which

Questions/Ideas

NOTES:

Summary/Reflection/Other

are related to Art and the Arts and Entertainment industry. Based on these search results, one of the words that I would need to use, because it's one of the most discoverable, is the word "gallery" in my online written communications. By using the word "gallery" to help promote the XYZ Art Studio, I have a better chance of people finding the XYZ Art Studio when they type in the word "gallery" into a search engine. So that means I need that word embedded in my post and in my blogs and other marketing communications that are online.

So how do you put these three components all together?

With content!

First of all, you need to define your goals of what you need to convey in your messaging. That means you're setting the tone for your business or your organization and you want to make sure that you come across as authoritative and trustworthy. In your posts, remember you're going to keep them brief, but you need to make sure you have a graphic, maybe a trending topic, engaging text and a call to action.

Let me break that down a little further for you.

DEFINING YOUR GOALS-

In the easiest way possible, you're basically trying to persuade people to buy or to use your product (or your service or your organization, etc.). You need to tell people to do that. Yes, they actually need to be told; therefore, you need to include a call to action: (ie: "So call now! 555-555-5555", would be one way post a call to action). A "Sign up today!" would be another way of showing a call of action. Those sorts of words tell the follower exactly what you expect them to do by reading your post.

Whenever possible, include a link. Especially if it's a link back to your website. If you haven't picked up on it yet, that's a really important thing to do that helps boost your website. Content should also be something people want to share with other people and a resource that people will go back to.

Remember to do your preliminary keyword search. That doesn't mean you

Questions/Ideas

NOTES:

Summary/Reflection/Other

need to do this every single time you are putting out a post. Because oftentimes you're going to do a keyword search, and then you'll know which keywords are your primary words for your business. The main point is, you want to know which keywords your target audience would be using, so you can be found by them.

Then be sure to align your goals and your keyword types with the right content:

- Great content that's suited for your audience
- Focus your on-page optimization efforts with keywords
- Promote that content at the right time
- Guide the visitor with your content. (In other words, encourage them to make an appointment with you, buy something from you, contact you, or sign up for something that you need them to sign up for). You get the picture.

AD POST HACKS-(Aka: More Pro Tips/Reminders so your post gets more attention)

- Be sure to add a "!"
- Use a short title in all caps
- ALWAYS use an image
- If you are offering something for free, make sure you add the word "FREE" (in caps)!
- Focus on positive words and refrain from negatives
- Some also believe in the power of emojis
    - Use in the top line, in the middle and near the end of a post (See the following example)

Questions/Ideas

NOTES:

Summary/Reflection/Other

Join us for our next
Success Guest

LET'S TALK SHOP WITH

Deanna Irish
WineTourDrivers.com

Your Ad Has a High Relevance Score
Great work! Your ad has an average relevance score of 5, which means
it's getting more positive feedback and is costing less to deliver than
most ads on Facebook.

3,489   884
People Reached   Engagements   Boost Again

Boosted on Aug 21, 2019   Completed
By Misha Tabor Giacomini

People   Post
Reached   2.5K   Engagement   775

View Results

BOS   4 Comments 6 Shares

Questions/Ideas

NOTES:

Summary/Reflection/Other

ANALYTICS-

Overtime the more you post, you're going to be able to start reviewing your analytics. This is really important because it will help drive when, where, and what you use for your marketing communications.

- Analytics will share with you the following and more:
- Traffic
- Reach
- Audio
- Content analysis
- Competitive benchmarking! (Yes, that means you can keep an eye on your competitors and how their posts are doing)!

Following are some sample dashboard of analytics you will want to review monthly for your social media:

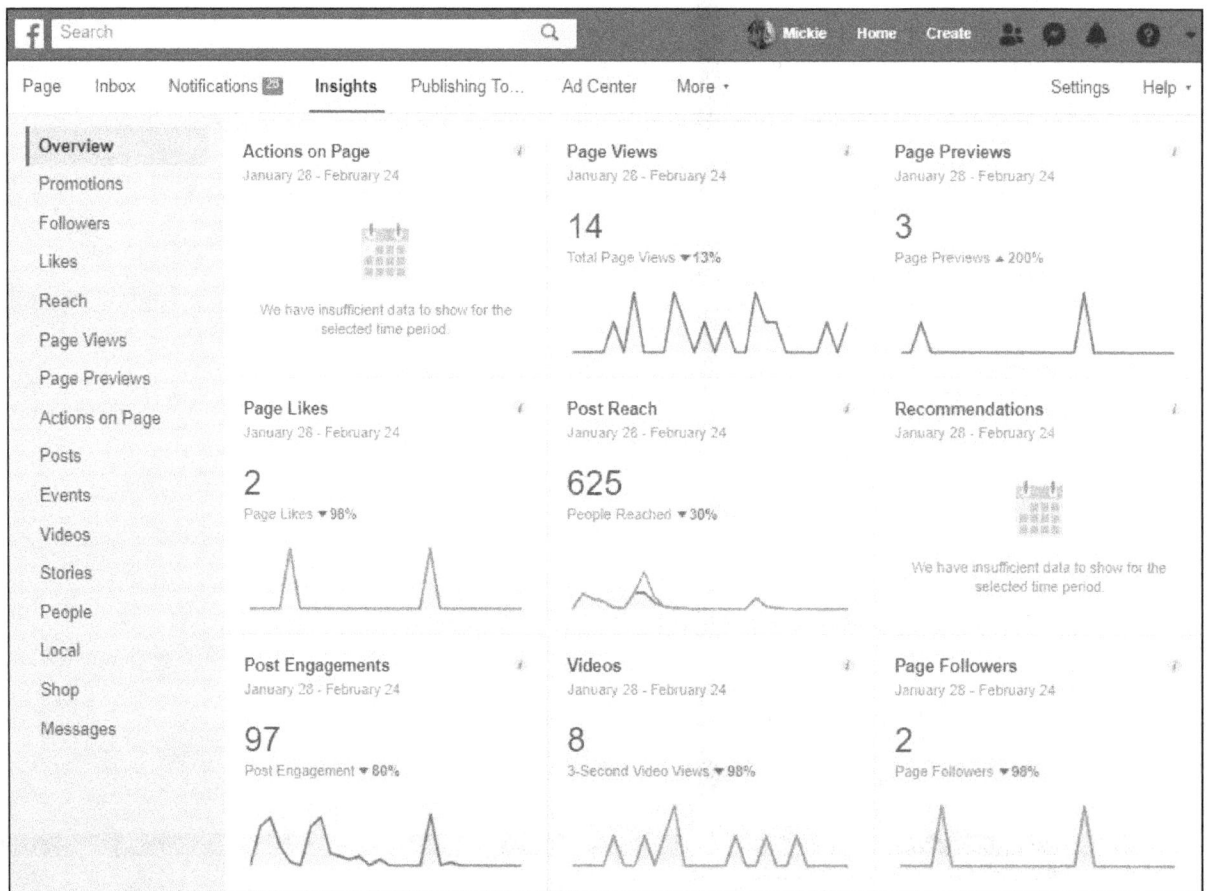

Questions/Ideas | NOTES:

Summary/Reflection/Other

So why is this important?

Analytics are important because they will help you with determining when you're most likely to reach your target audience, and who your audience is that you're reaching with your posts.

You might have some "sleeper niches" out there that you never knew about!

Bottom line is by tracking your analytics, it helps you drive your marketing dollars and time, and in the long run it saves you time and money, (Because you won't be wasting it on areas that are not effective).

REACH-

It's important for you to seek out on your analytics what your reach is. Basically, that means studying your posts' statistics and discovering who the people are that are actually reading your posts. That's important because it really does shape who your target audience is on THAT particular social media platform.

HUH? What do you mean by "THAT" particular social media platform?

You could be using Facebook and Instagram and your audience may very well be very different for both. So that helps guide how you design your posts for future postings on your various social media to grab the most attention.

In other words, you're not going to use the same post on Facebook as you would on Instagram, if you find that your target audience on Facebook is 45 to 60 year old women, and that your target audience on Instagram is trending as 20 to 30 year old men. Right?

Questions/Ideas

NOTES:

Summary/Reflection/Other

So this is really critical to know, because you want to design posts that are going to actually be engaging for your target audience on each platform. This does not happen overnight. It takes time and a lot of posts for the analytics to start telling you a story about who your followers are.

Be patient.

You won't even be looking at analytics for a full month after regular posting. (And this also serves as another good reason why less is more when you are a beginner).

Following is an example of what analytics could possibly show you. In particular, this screenshot is for who your fans and followers are on Facebook:

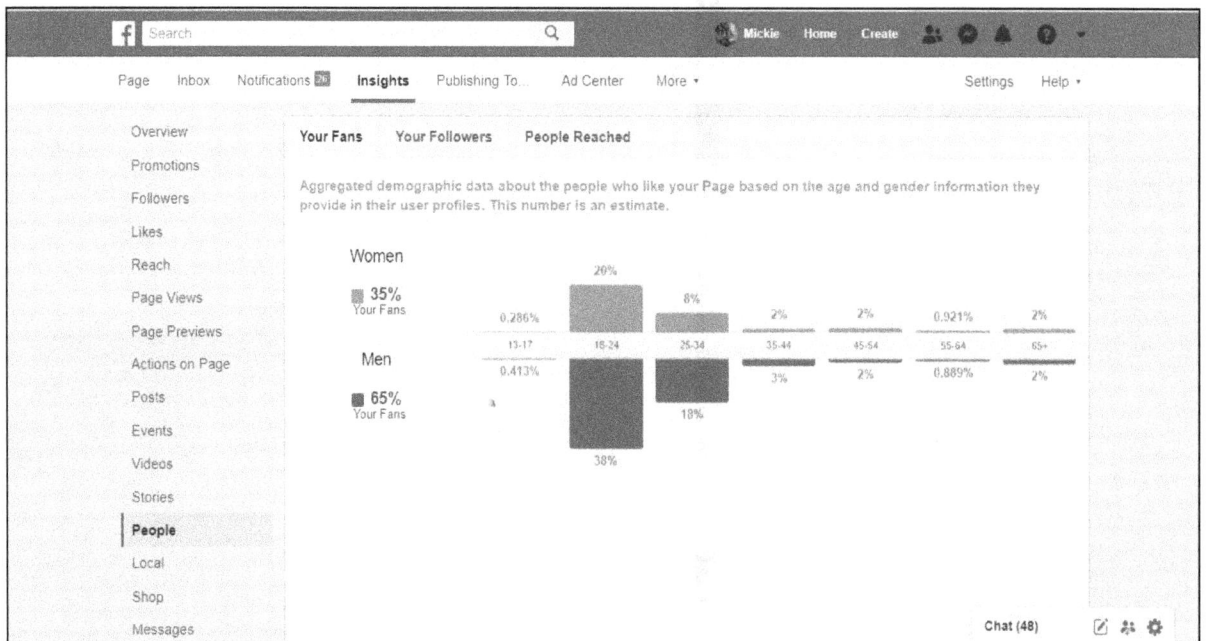

Questions/Ideas   NOTES:

Summary/Reflection/Other

They can even show you WHERE your fans and followers live:

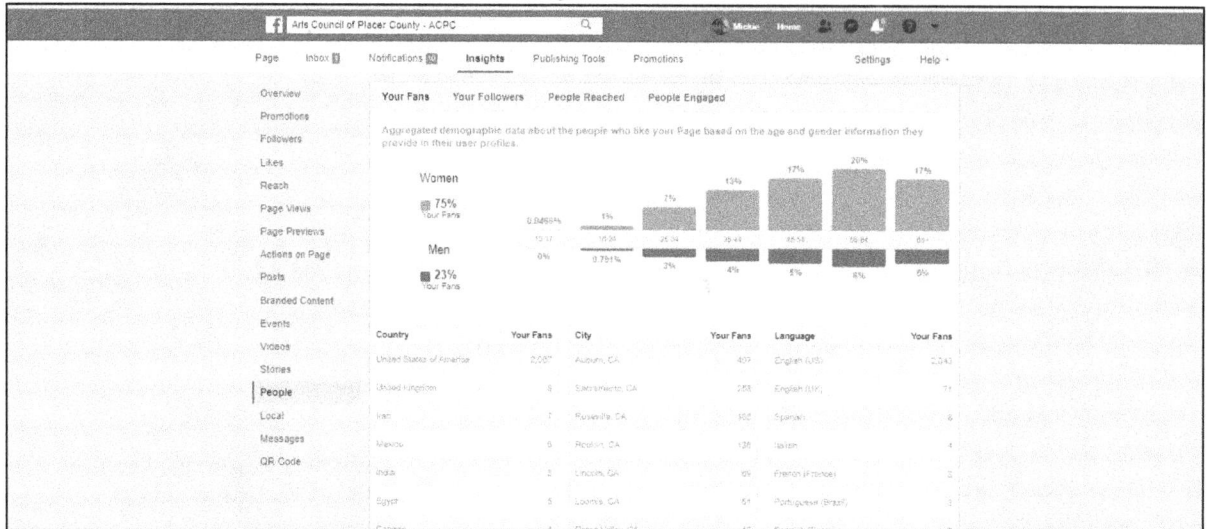

Personally, I find that knowing which days (and times of the day) to post are the most important analytics I could possibly use:

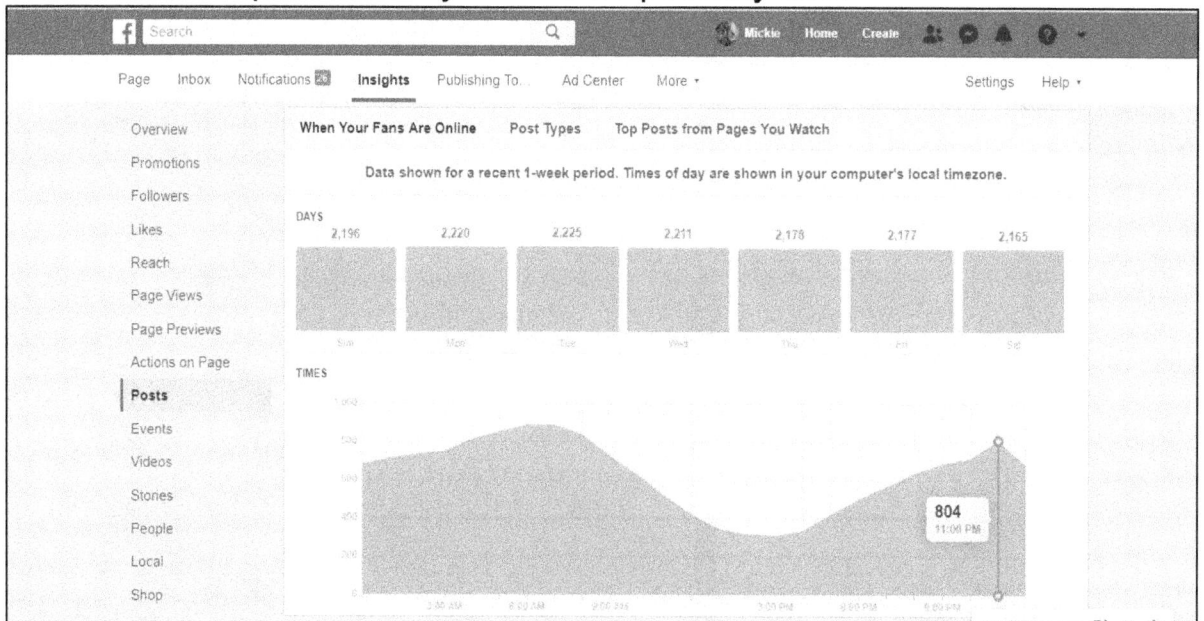

<u>That's the end of Lesson 3! For homework over the next week</u>:
- Continue practicing writing and scheduling your posts. Let's kick it up now to 5 posts for Facebook, with images.
- Also look up the keywords that go with your business, and be sure to add two into EACH of your posts.

Questions/Ideas

NOTES:

Summary/Reflection/Other

- On two of your posts, be sure to add your website link.
- Curate 2 articles, post them, and add them to your social media library! Seriously! Be sure you are building your social media library! I often write some generic posts that can be used at any time during the year, but also keep posts in my library that may be used at certain times of the year (holidays, etc).
- If you haven't already, set up your LinkedIn profile, so that when people meet you, they may connect with you through LinkedIn. I am not asking you to do this to post out, (especially if this is not your target audience), I am recommending you do this because it adds credibility to you as a business owner/professional because you can be found on LinkedIn (and what it describes under your profile matches with your business, etc.) It's a psychological thing, and if it ends in a sale, or something else, it will be worth it. Right?

Questions/Ideas | NOTES:

Summary/Reflection/Other

Lesson FOUR:
OTHER NO TO LOW COST WAYS TO MARKET

This lesson is going to expand past digital marketing with additional ideas that you may be able to incorporate to market your business or project. While some will be able to be used in conjunction with your digital marketing campaigns, most will be a break from having to think "online." That said, let me take a moment to make it very clear, Social Media is a huge presence in our daily lives. Almost everyone is on social media, so your business should be too!

In addition to having your website, your Facebook Business page, (and other business social media pages, if conducive to your business), it's very important to incorporate the following as part of your marketing strategy:

Email Marketing (eblasts)

Write a POS guide book

Design infographics

Outreach events and opportunities

Create a YouTube video

Vehicle Branding

Business Partnership

Local media

Marketing to existing customers

and let's circle back to...

....your website, right? (Because every single business needs a website I canNOT make that any more clear than that)!

Questions/Ideas

NOTES:

Summary/Reflection/Other

EMAIL MARKETING-

A critical component of any marketing strategy campaign is utilizing advertising in the form of e-blast and/or electronic newsletters. Of course this means you need to be capturing your clients' and potential clients'/customers' email addresses so that you may send them these amazing e-blasts that you are going to be creating to share your great information and the reasons why they need to be coming in/contacting you and buying your (*insert item/service/etc. here*).

I recommend a few programs out there that really help with sending out your e-blasts. They read your database exports of your email database lists and they help make your emails looks amazing! Furthermore, it doesn't take a whole lot of extra work to have a great professional e-blast, so do it! It's free! (At least at this at the time of this writing it is). Two of the ones that I highly recommend are MailChimp and Constant Contact. They're both essentially the same, in principle, it's just a personal preference really.

Every time somebody contacts you, buys from you, has an inquiry from you, etc., be sure to capture their email addresses and add them to your email list. The great thing about utilizing a program such as MailChimp or Constant Comment is that if these people want off your email list, they are able to say "unsubscribe me," so no harm, no foul, right?

Some of the things you should be sending out in your email blasts are discounts, coupons, updates, news, previews, etc.

The one thing to definitely keep in mind, however, is to be sure not to over send! We all know how it is when we get bombarded by the same company, or person, with two or three emails every flipping day, and it makes us insane, so we unsubscribe. You don't want your customers to unsubscribe you, so don't over inundate their email and you have a better chance of keeping them on your eblast list. However, you still want to make a regular practice of staying in their mind, so be sure to do at least a monthly e-blast but no more than once a week in order not to become that annoying individual that they unsubscribe. It's all about balance.

PRO TIP: Start a customer referral program (give out a free product or discounts for sending new customers. It doesn't have to be huge or

Questions/Ideas

NOTES:

Summary/Reflection/Other

expensive. Sometimes just a little recognition goes a long way)!

BLOGS-

What are blogs?

I always tell people to think of a blog as a website that hosts a bunch of their articles, per se. For you, these articles can serve as marketing tools!!! We are going to talk about this much more soon in Lesson 5. For now, just keep in the back of your mind that they are very important.

WEBSITES-

I cannot stress enough that every single small business needs a website! And as earlier mentioned, when people do a web search for your business, your website should show up at the top of the results. WHY? Simple. So they don't go to one of your competitors whose website ranked up higher. Your website either serves as an extension storefront for your brick and mortar business, OR it is the storefront for your e-commerce. So it is important.

This is also an area I recommend you do not skimp on. While it is okay to put a basic website up for the moment, or hire a teenager to do it, you really need to consider spending your marketing dollars on having one professionally designed. (Think about when you see a business with a temporary banner sign on a storefront, until that establishment gets their permanent professional one. That's the same thing here. You need to establish a professional presence with your website, and send a message that you are the real deal).

POS GUIDEBOOKS-

POS stands for Point of Sale. So a guidebook is a book, oftentimes written as a step-by-step guide that touches on a process of your business. (Example: DIY Marketing for Beginners, etc.) What's great about POS, is that you set them up so that they are sold through an outfit like Amazon, and then they are printed when purchased and sent out directly to the client. No inventory! That's right, no muss, no fuss! YAY!

Questions/Ideas

NOTES:

Summary/Reflection/Other

INFOGRAPHICS-

If you aren't sure what these look like, Google it for more examples. Here's one for now:

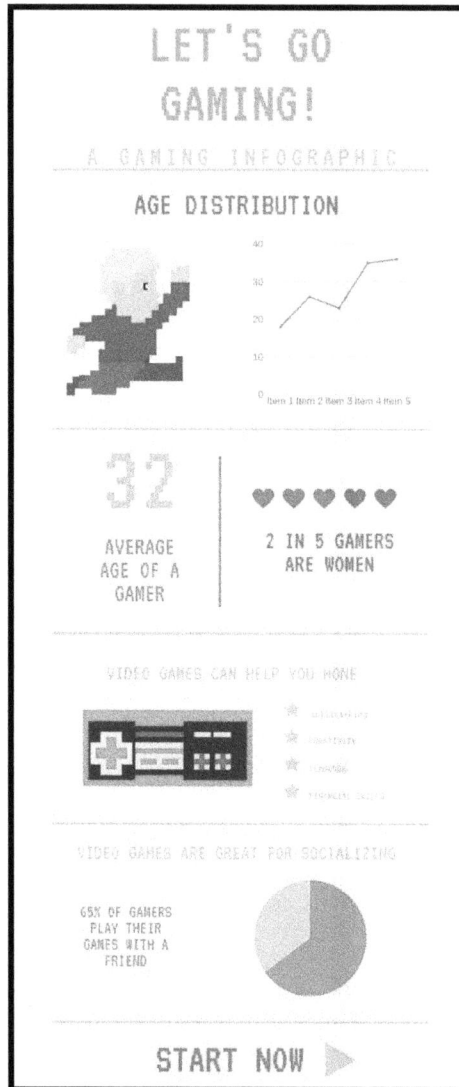

When would I design an Infographic?

Infographics are a great way to illustrate data related to a concept of/about your business. People will pay more attention if you have graphics/photos, etc. to illustrate the data you wish to share. They are well worth the time to create too, because you may use them in a bunch of your stuff: website, social media, brochures & media kits, just to name a few!

Questions/Ideas   NOTES:

Summary/Reflection/Other

OUTREACH EVENTS-

Get connected with your community!

A great way to maximize exposure is to participate in community events. Trade Shows are great too, but tend to be more costly than community events. Also, if you are truly part of a non-profit organization, sometimes community events will offer you a discount for your booth.

Speaking engagements are also a great way to increase your exposure. Anytime you are invited to speak at an event, meeting, etc. you should be jumping at the chance to do it. This is free publicity and an opportunity to have a captive audience who is invited to listen to you and how great your business, etc. is!

Along the line of speaking, being a radio station guest or tv guest is another chance to broadcast to mass amounts of people how terrific you are, for free!!! Think about it. Many people pay for tv/radio advertising, and it is quite costly and very difficult to gauge effectiveness. Further, it is only for a very short sport, usually 15 or 30 seconds. But when you are an invited guest to discuss whatever it is you do, you get to have all that exposure to all those viewers/listeners, for longer and for free. Need I say more?

Joining professional and/or business organizations is an excellent opportunity to network with others. This is great, because the people you meet may be very mindful about using services, as exclusively as possible, from others within the group, and they may also recommend you to other people outside the organizations. So always bring a ton of business cards to these events!

A great site to tune into is Meet-up.com. This site is overflowing with all sorts of different groups. Start by looking for networking groups who meet regularly in your area, and then start trying to find groups where you would be a great addition and many of the members might become a customer/client. It is all about networking, networking, networking.

Speaking of networking, I also encourage you to participate in local business mixers.

Questions/Ideas

NOTES:

Summary/Reflection/Other

YOUTUBE-

Being on video might not be your thing, but creating a video could help you promote your business.

How?

Make it relevant to your business. Share a video of something that helps people, and builds your credibility. I like to share this analogy. Let's pretend for example that you are a plumber. You could create a video showing people how to fix the the floaty thingamabob in the toilet talk, or maybe you are a painter, and you teach some basic paint strokes, or an auto mechanic walking people through the importance of changing the fluids in their vehicle. You aren't giving away the store by doing this, but you are building trust and credibility so that when they have a bigger plumbing issue, or want to learn how to really paint, or have car problems, they will be thinking of you! Plus, you may add the video to your website, for people to reference & watch when surfing your site.

BUSINESS PARTNERSHIPS-

Cross-promotion helps cut down on the cost of advertising and can create valuable synergies that benefit all the partners.

I recommend that you team up with other local businesses:

Cross-promote each other's businesses

- Think cross-promotion coupons that direct clients to each others' businesses
- Think promoting each others' businesses on your email distribution lists
- Look for a business to cross-promotion partner with that is complementary. (For example, an eye lash lounge and a nail salon or hair salon).
- Partner for events and split the costs by sharing space.

BRANDING & SIGNAGE-
It probably goes without saying, your company car needs to have signage.

Questions/Ideas | NOTES:

Summary/Reflection/Other

Full on paint jobs/wrap jobs can be a bit pricey, so if that is out of your budget, consider, at your own risk: magnets that stick the sides of your doors or even better, window decals that do not obstruct your vision.

If you have a brick and mortar place of business, be sure you have signage outside, and if there is pedestrian traffic, it is very important to have a sandwich board style sign pointing to the entrance to go in and buy, visit, sign up, etc. (Be sure there is an arrow, it is psychological, so be sure to add it). Announce some sort of sale, even if it isn't a discount, you can mention, "We have (insert object) today!" With an arrow pointing to the entrance. You could also announce new inventory, etc.

MEDIA RELATIONS-

Did you know that you can send press/new releases for free? It does cost you your time, but to email to the appropriate media outlets costs nothing, and could mean additional great exposure for you.

Here's the deal. The point that you have opened a new business is not necessarily newsworthy. So you need to think about an interesting angle of your business that might capture media interest. For example, let's say someone is opening their new optometry practice. Not so newsworthy, but if that optometrist is engaging in some sort of community outreach, like offering free eye exams to those in need for 50 people on a Saturday between Noon and 4pm, well that may be more of interest.

WHY?

It's the giving back to the community piece that they may want to do a story on. Guess what? Not only is that a great thing to do, but then the business also gets promoted, and the icing on the cake is that it also presents the optometrist as an upstanding member of the community--so it builds credibility, integrity and clout. That's not all! After the segment or article airs/publishes, that same optometrist can then take the link to the feature and put it out on all the business's social media platforms, send it out in an eblast, and keep it on the business website for future reference. All that advertising for FREE!!!

Questions/Ideas

NOTES:

Summary/Reflection/Other

More times than not, you will send out to your local media. (But depending on the story angle and sort of business/organization it is, it could go to national or even global outlets). Be sure to share out the unique or newsworthy happenings. You may even offer to do a series for them!

When possible, find ways to network with local reporters (without coming off as a stalker).

Keep in mind they will not cover promotional things (that is what paid advertising is for).

Involve the media in your grand openings, moves, or charity events (they may not be covering you directly, but you may be able to mention your venue as a satellite remote possibility at your event, and be sure there will be something unique happening at it). Think about when you see news trucks out on location, or radio stations set up all over town.

If you don't have a charity event happening anytime soon, put one together! Or sponsor someone else's charity and promote the heck out of the fact that your business is part of it. Try to get the charity to add you as a sponsor on all their media spots/ad placements.

LIKES & FOLLOWS-

We like LIKES, and when it comes to our business page, we certainly want people following us around!

Here are some strategies to increase your LIKES/FOLLOWS:

- Include social media engagement buttons on site
- Promote your Facebook/Instagram, etc. pages offline
- Modify your Facebook url to look more branded
- Invite people you know
- Add admins for temporary and invite people they know
- When boosting posts, click on who is liking your post and invite them to follow you
- Offer a small discount or freebie for people who like your page
- Promote engaging articles/posts

Questions/Ideas

NOTES:

Summary/Reflection/Other

- Cross-promote your other social media platforms
- Cross-promote with partners
- Promote a contest
- Post videos...
  ...and when all else fails, post a cute dog photo! LOL!

Be sure you have your Facebook Page verified that you are a legit business. To do this, (at the time of this writing), go to SETTINGS, and click on VERIFY THE PAGE under Page Verification:

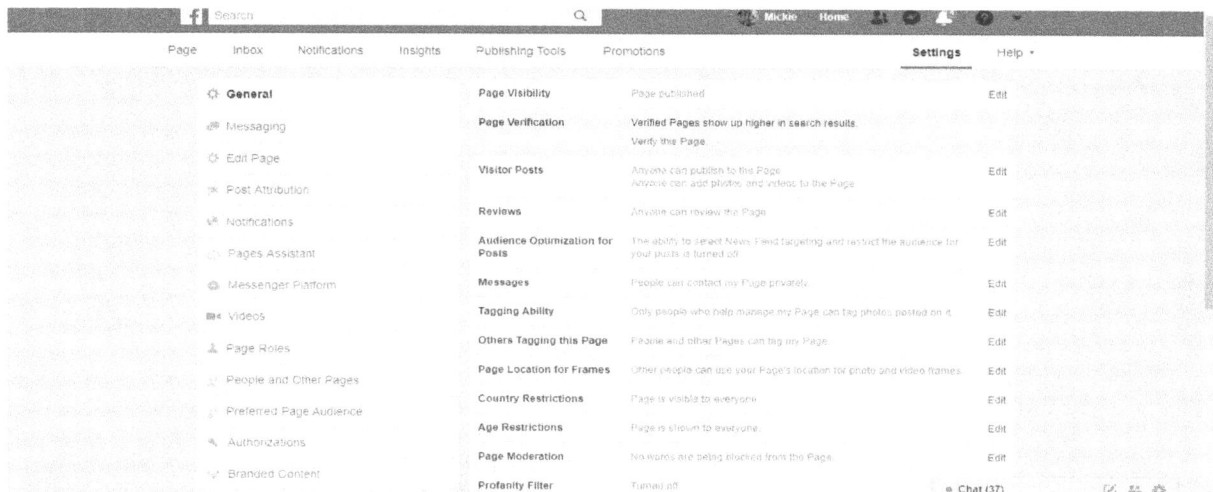

You will need to enter your business phone number for this. If it doesn't work they will ask for some sort of documents that prove you are legit.

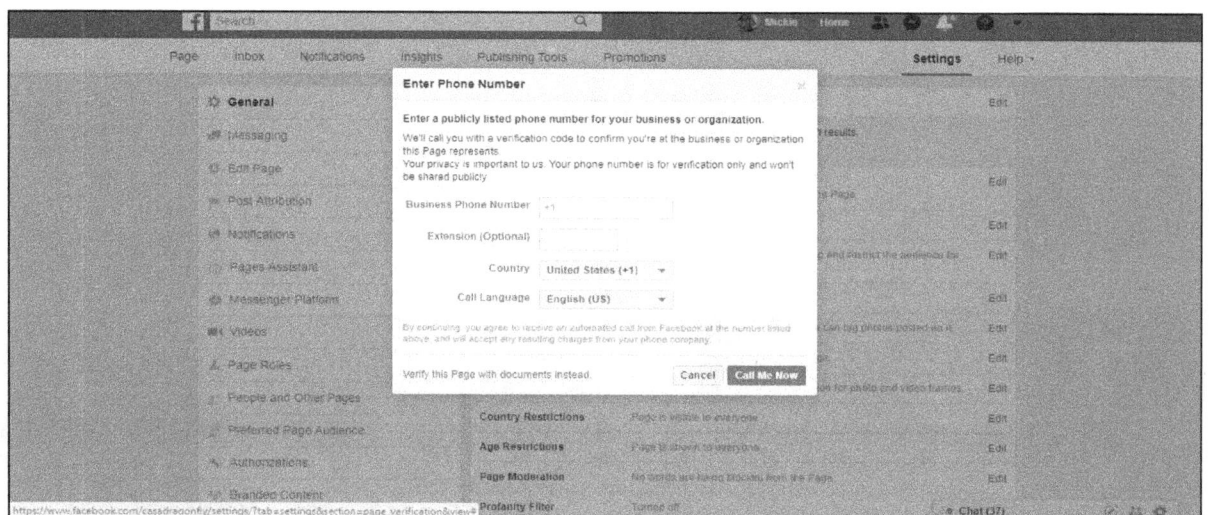

Questions/Ideas | NOTES:

Summary/Reflection/Other

To become more branded looking on your Facebook page, go to the ABOUT section and under User Name add your business name. If it is taken, find something very close.

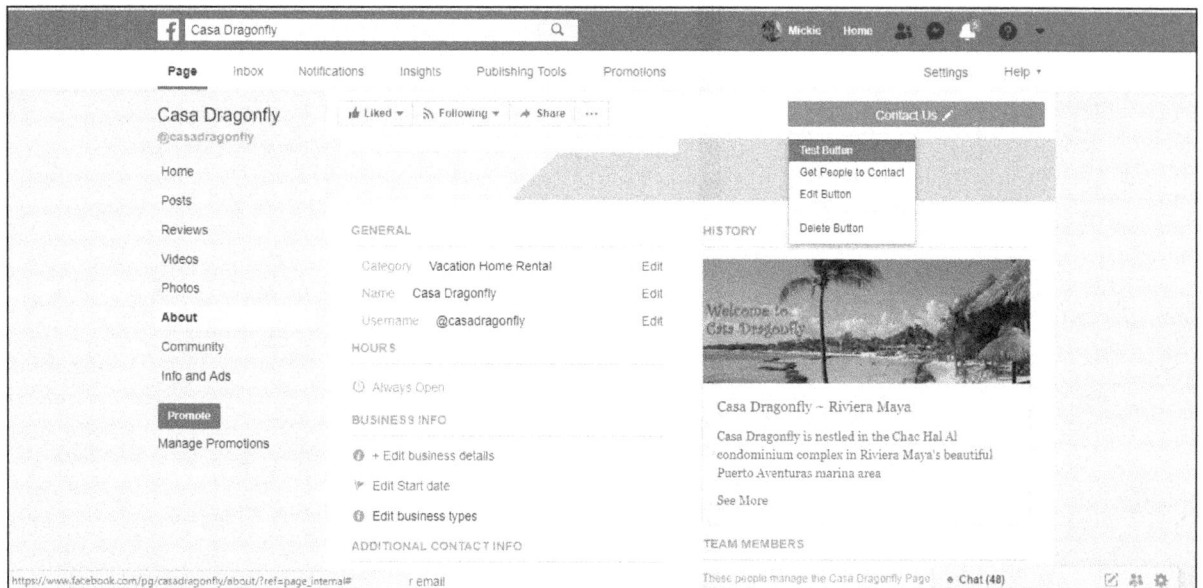

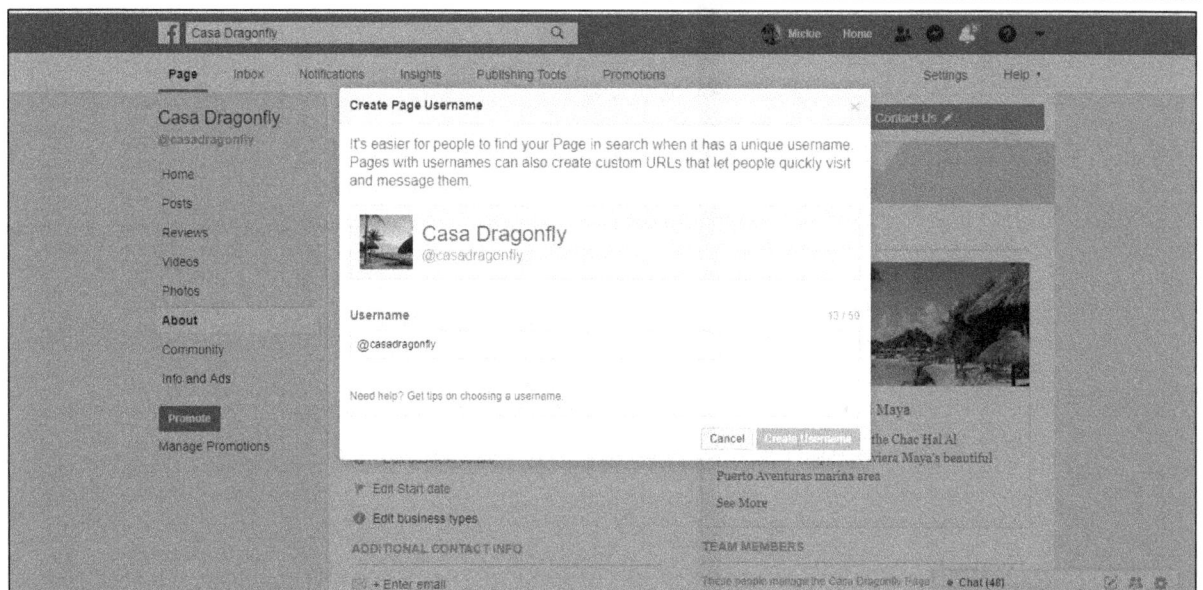

Last, look at all your posts that have some sort of LIKE engagement. Click on the LIKE to see who has liked your post.

Questions/Ideas

NOTES:

Summary/Reflection/Other

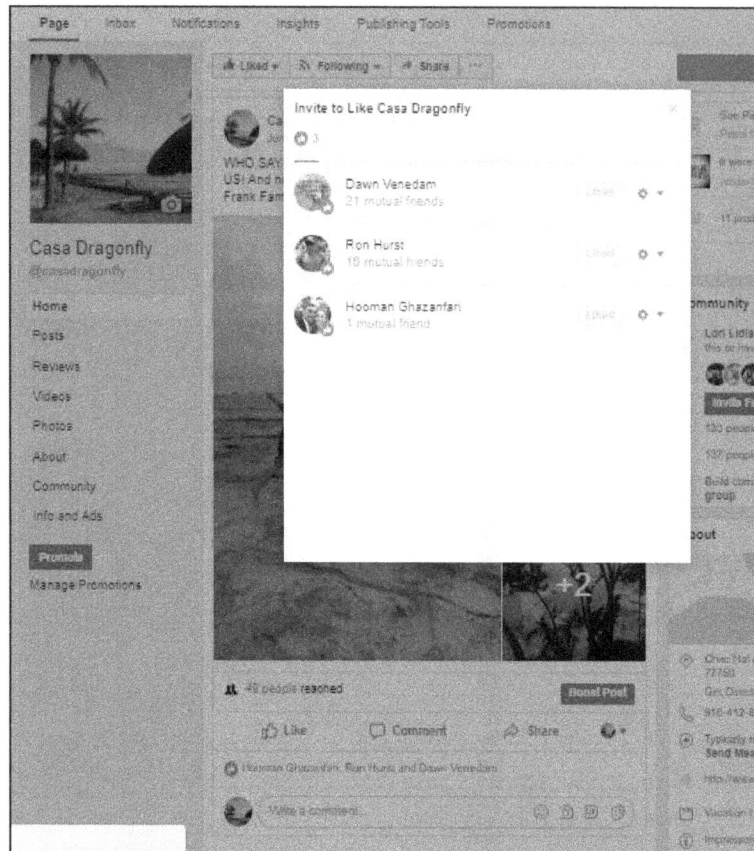

Where you see the faint like box above, it will say INVITE if they haven't liked your page yet. If that is the case, simply click on it and FB will send an invite to that person to LIKE your page. (This is a trick that even many advanced professional digital marketers don't know--but now YOU do!)

The most important part of marketing your business are these three key elements:

Be the authority (of whatever it is you do)
Be trustworthy
Be full of integrity

When people have a choice between you and someone else to do business with, if you are shady or dishonest, clients/customers will do a hard pass on you, in order to do business with someone who they believe has integrity and they can trust. Even if you are the ultimate expert on whatever it is you do, if you come across as someone who has a lack of integrity, they will run to the business who has integrity. Wouldn't you?

Questions/Ideas | NOTES:

Summary/Reflection/Other

People want to know that you know your stuff, but trustworthiness and integrity will win them over every time.

That's the end of Lesson 4, let's bring on the homework! For the next week, do the following:

- Write 3 Posts for Facebook for this week and schedule, and write 3 for the following week and schedule! (6 in total)
- Curate 6 photos/graphics for Facebook that you may use also with your other Social Media platforms, that will go with the above posts.
- Curate 10 articles and add to your Social Media Library
- Then, make a list of potential businesses you might be able to partner with for cross-promotion (it's okay to have more than one partner)! Reach out to the top three that would make the best sense to partner with and share that you've been taking this course and you've been encouraged to reach out to them for cross-promotion opportunities.
- Next, make sure you have set up your Facebook page to look more branded. (This is important to do before your next homework assignment).
- Last, after making sure you have a "branded" Facebook link, create an eblast to share out to your email distribution list. (I recommend that your eblast touches on your new Facebook business page and that you invite them to LIKE/FOLLOW it. Be sure you include the new branded link).

Questions/Ideas

NOTES:

Summary/Reflection/Other

Lesson FIVE:
BLOGGING, WEBSITES & MORE

In this lesson we will discuss:
- Why blogging?
- Maximizing a blog post
- Websites
- More Digital Marketing via Banner Ads

BLOGGING-
First of all, what is a blog & why should you do it?

In the simplest terms, a blog is an article on a website. Many times the "blog" is a dedicated website devoted solely to the blog articles on the site. However, many businesses will add a blog tab to their business website, so that the article may "live" there along with the other pages of information on the business website. This is my recommendation, because blogging is just one more great way to help drive traffic to your on-line storefront.

Most people set up these pages to write articles, stories, etc. But others use blogging to post their photos, art, etc.

When a blogger gains a lot of followers, they often will become bloggists and monetize their site for addition revenue.

In my humble, yet professional opinion, blogging is one of the most effective ways to create content for your social media platforms. The reason why is because you will be writing articles about the things your clients/customers need/want to know about.

Then you will maximize these articles by breaking them up into mini posts, but always inserting the link for people to go to your website and read the original story in its entirety. A great way to do this is to write articles that are easy to break apart, such as: 3 ways to..., 5 Steps for…, 7 Musts for…, etc. The reason this works so well is that you may then create a brief post each day on a different way/step/must, etc., and again, always add the link to drive your followers to your website to read the rest of your story. Think of it this way, once they are on your website, they are inside your on-line "store." So the aim is that they read the story and then browse the rest of

Questions/Ideas

NOTES:

Summary/Reflection/Other

your site and buy, etc. (whatever it is that you are wanting them to do).

For starters, you should be writing one to two blogs a week, and remember to rotate these through your social media library to reuse in the future. (That said, be mindful of keeping your blog article rather timeless, so you may use and reuse over and over again). One blog article can easily give you 3-4 posts on your social media, maybe more. So it is a great investment of your time!

Many of my clients are often overwhelmed by the prospect of needing to write a blog for their business, but some of the greatest bloggers have this to say:

"Don't focus on having a great blog. Focus on <u>producing a blog that's great for your readers</u>.

As a blogger, everything that you do flows from understanding your audience and <u>seeking to help</u> them as much as possible." **~Brian Clark**

"Blogging is a conversation, not a code." **~Mike Butcher**

"A blog is only as interesting as the interest shown in others." **~Lee Odden**

So the point is, don't stress, just do your best!

Following is an example of how Casa Dragonfly works through DayTripper Magazine, (a travel blog, essentially), to maximize exposure:

Questions/Ideas | NOTES:

Summary/Reflection/Other

First, there is an article for the website:

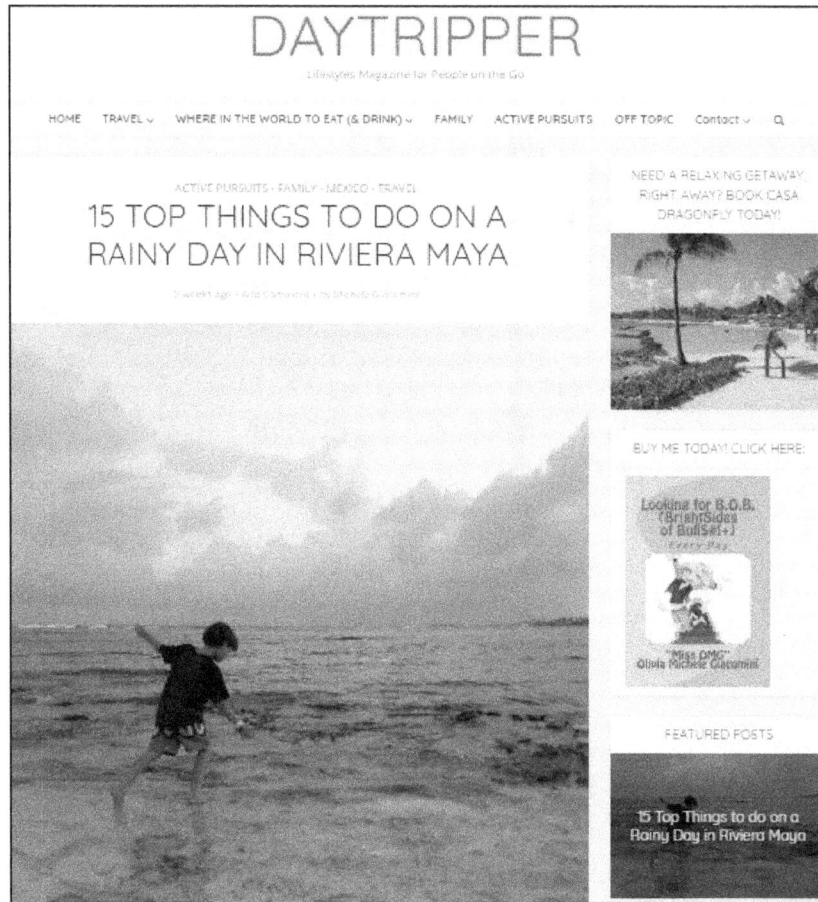

Then a post is used on social media to grab attention and drive traffic to the website. Other posts can be made throughout the week on a few of the tips a day, and then followers may click on the link to read the whole article on the website:

Questions/Ideas

NOTES:

Summary/Reflection/Other

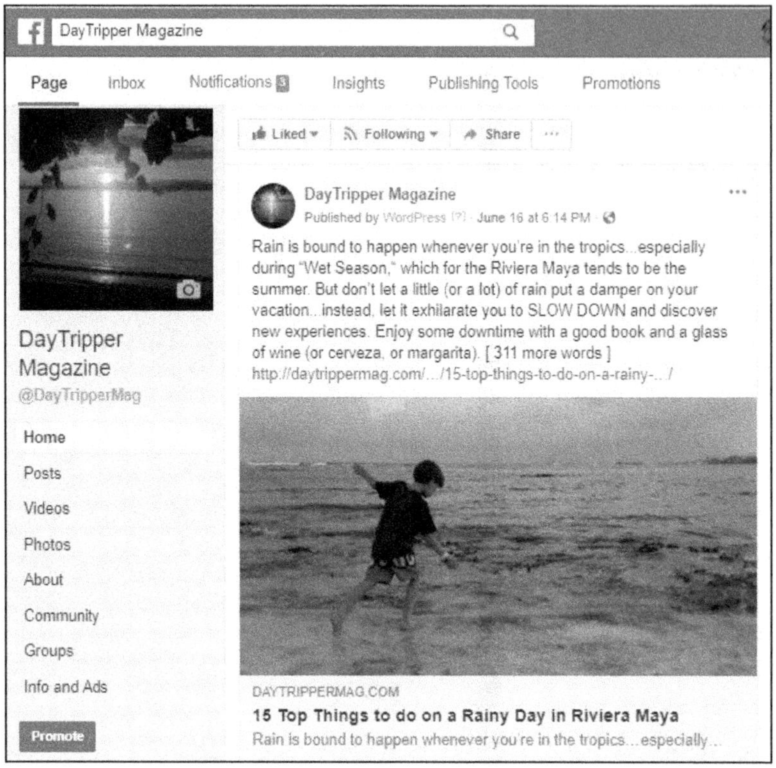

Another example shows an article about restaurants:

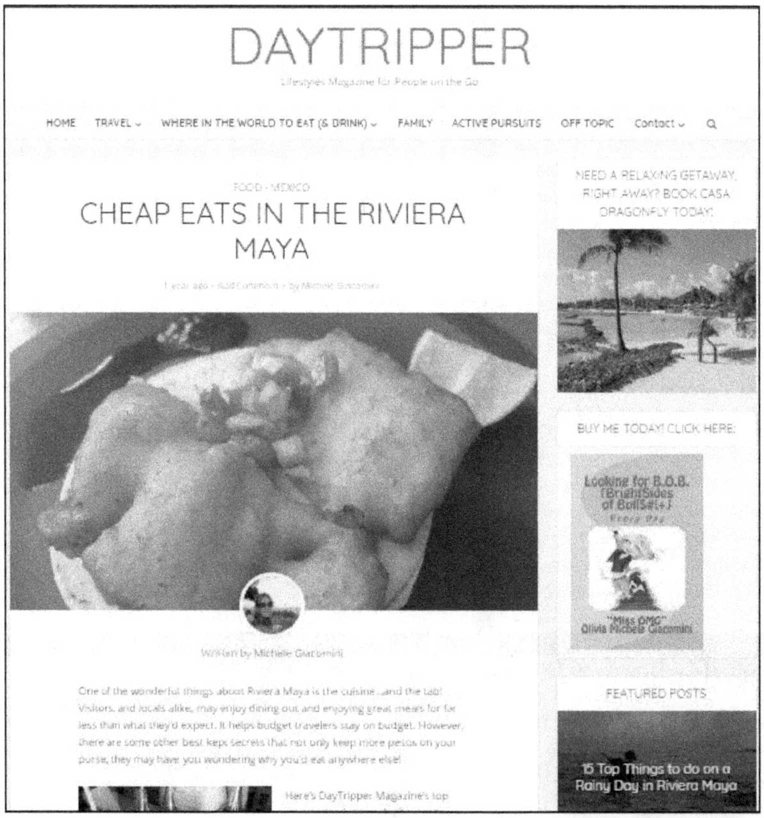

Questions/Ideas

NOTES:

Summary/Reflection/Other

This article was on several restaurants in the area near Casa Dragonfly's Mexico location. Then social media posts were created to talk about one restaurant per day and drive traffic to the website, plus a post about the whole article, again linking people to the website.

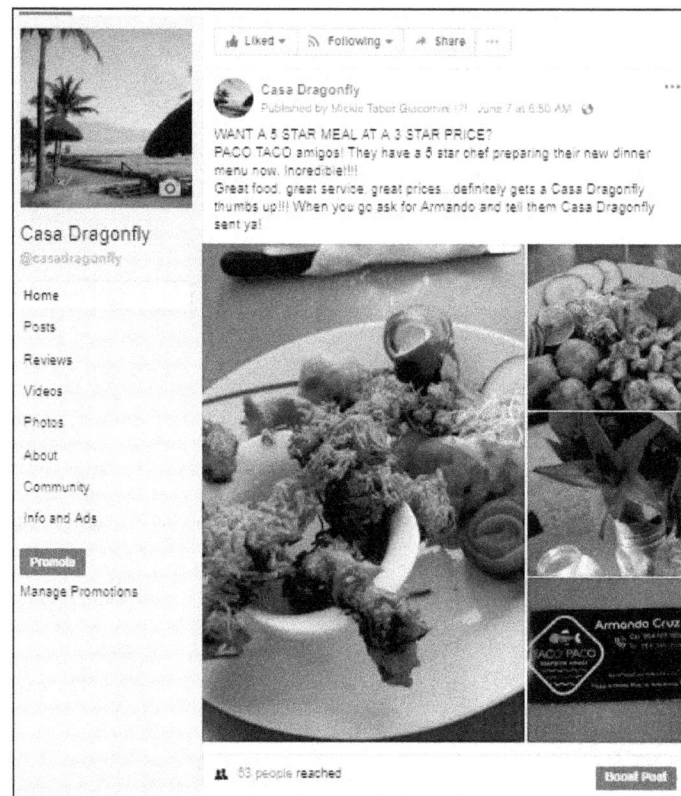

As I mentioned, you can really maximize the use of a blog, so let's review this again, because this is really important:

Once you write your blog article, **REPURPOSE IT**!

First: Use it on your website

Second: Break it apart into mini sections & post on social media...always linking back to your full article on your website

Third: Look for ways to manipulate for an additional article (Top 5 Ways..., 3 Tips to..., A Quick Fix for...)

Questions/Ideas

NOTES:

Summary/Reflection/Other

Last: Add it all to your Social Media Library to use again in a few months!

Got it? Good! Now go write a blog article!

But where can I do this blog thing?

#1 I recommend on your business website. If you don't have a website, set up a blog page and cross promote with your social media. I recommend Blogger for beginners, as it is very easy to use.

#2 Once you are super savvy with Blogger, then you can make the leap over to WordPress or Wix. If you go with WordPress it is important that you use the WordPress.org (not ".com") site, as it will offer more for you as you become more advanced with your skills.

Need more convincing?

Review my 7 reasons why you should be blogging for your business:

1)   It drives traffic to your website!
2)   It helps convert that traffic into leads
3)   It helps establish authority
4)   It drives long term results
5)   It keeps your community informed
6)   It helps to improve your writing & getting creativity going
7)   It's a no to low cost way to expand your marketing strategy!

So we've talked about driving traffic to your website. This means you may be able to convert those visitors to your site into leads which may turn into sales, etc. It also helps you establish yourself as an authority on the topic for whatever your business is. Many believe this type of traffic drives long term results and may encourage visitors to return frequently to your site, because they want to read your blog articles!

You should also consider that you are doing your business's community a service by keeping your clients and potential clients well-informed.

If you are apprehensive, keep in mind that writing is like anything, the more

Questions/Ideas

NOTES:

Summary/Reflection/Other

you do it, the better you get!

And did I mention it's FREE if you DIY???

(PLEASE NOTE: Next up are some important, yet <u>NOT</u> "no to low cost," marketing tools I'd be remiss not to share).

WEBSITES-

Will I wither without a website?

Yes. Why yes you will. YOU NEED A WEBSITE.

Remind me WHY?

Every small business needs a website. When people do a web search for your business, your website should show up at the top of the results.

If people are looking for products or services in your area, your web page should be among the results. You can improve your website's chances of showing up in search results through SEO.

So, what makes a website effective? **Your business information must be clear.** People should be able to easily find your location, hours, and contact information. Your website should at least have basic information about your products or services. You might also have customer testimonials (and a blog!!!).

Ok, okay! I get it, but how do I GET it?

You can build your own website. But this is one area where I would highly recommend you spend your marketing dollars and have it professionally done. Think of it as an investment in your business. It is your online storefront, so image is EVERYTHING!

If you've never built one, hire out for sure! But first, be sure to contact a professional agency to help you design your business logo if you don't have one. (Like ours)! Your logo will be on everything, so you need it for branding every little thing, and especially your website!

Questions/Ideas   NOTES:

Summary/Reflection/Other

Still wondering if a website is right for you? Here are my Top 10 reasons why you need one:

1. It tells people who and where you are
2. It's global
3. People may access 24/7 at their own leisure
4. Offers instant communication
5. Fairly inexpensive compared to most advertising techniques
6. Attracts new customers
7. Helps improve Customer Service
8. Helps you collect data about your customers & leads
9. People love shopping online
10. Fairly easy to maintain

DIGITAL BANNER ADS-(Advanced Beginner stuff here)!

What are these? Why are they needed? Are they free?

When you surf the internet, think about the ads that pop up. Often times these are banner ads. Banner advertising is also called "display advertising" (and they are visual in nature because they are not just text, they also include creative images).

The purpose of banner advertising is to promote a brand. The banner ad can take the visitor from the host website to the advertiser's website or a specific landing page. Banner ads are intended to generate traffic to a website by linking to it. Also, web banners can function as regular, print advertisements: inform, notify about a new product, increase brand awareness, and so on.

You can start a banner advertising campaign with Google Adwords or any other display network.

The bad news is that they are NOT free; however, the great news is they can be super effective in many ways. One advantage of the online advertising over the traditional ones is that its effectiveness can be easily measured. The main effectiveness indicator is the **click-through rate**. The

Questions/Ideas

NOTES:

Summary/Reflection/Other

click-through rate is calculated by dividing the number of users who clicked on the ad by the number of times the ad was displayed (impressions).

Here are some other ways they are effective:

1) Digital banners complete your branding circle-TV/RADIO/PRINT cannot track like a digital banner ad

2) Generally less expensive than TV/RADIO/PRINT advertising

3) It captures your market! (So you can remarket & retarget)

4) Promotes an image of authority

5) Zero in on promotion: when, where, who

6) Get ads on relevant sites

Anything else?

Digital Marketing (Banner ads)
    I highly recommend digital ads that hit your target audience through on-line publications of THEIR interest.

(Can run roughly about $600+ for a tow week in depth campaign, but can provide amazing information)!

IT'S A GREAT INVESTMENT!

That's it! That is the end of Lesson 5 and this beginner's introduction to DIY marketing course. You need to keep up your regular routine (basically a repeat Week 4's) and this week add:

- Blog article writing

You've got this!

If you are looking for additional coaching, or help with logo design, website design and other marketing services, you may contact us at:

info.DragonflyRanch@gmail.com
www.TheDragonflyRanch.com

For specific coaching areas:
www.TheDragonflyRanch.com/business-coaching

For upcoming workshops, speaking events, and webinars:
www.TheDragonflyRanch.com/new-services

Author's Note:

I hope this book has been able to guide through the foundation of marketing your small business, start-up, project, etc. At times, marketing and promoting yourself can be overwhelming. But be productive, be positive, & be persistent through this adventure.

YOU GOT THIS!

About the author

O. Michele Giacomini is a writer, educator, business owner and a promoter of others. With over 14 years of business experience, PLUS, over 19 years working in the education industry & professional development, she has much to contribute to help bolster the success of others. When she isn't writing for a variety of publications, as well as her humorous Miss OMG books, you can find her coaching others for success in careers, business, writing/publishing and organizational strategies—or tending to her chickens on the country property she shares with her husband, in Northern California.

You can follow her on Facebook at:
https://www.facebook.com/TheDragonflyRanch/
https://www.facebook.com/OMGMissOMG/
and/or join the Success Networking FB page for her success vlog:
https://www.facebook.com/LetsTalkShopShow/

Follow her on LinkedIn: O. Michele Giacomini
_____

Other books by Olivia Michele Giacomini (Miss OMG):

Looking for B.O.B. (BrightSides of Bull$#!+): Every Day

https://www.amazon.com/dp/153085721X

Surviving the Holidays: HELL-i-DAZE

https://www.amazon.com/Surviving-Holidays-Olivia-Michele-Giacomini/dp/0578438399

Finding It: Your One Week Guide to Job Seeking Success

https://www.amazon.com//dp/0578504413

Springboard Back to Success: Your One Week Guide toward Finding Job Seeking Success

https://www.amazon.com//dp/1733036601

WHO WANTS A FREEBIE???

Check out my 30 favorite marketing tips for tight business budgets!

Go to this link here today:

http://bit.ly/MY30FAV

"I signed up for Dragonfly Ranch's beginning marketing class to pick up some helpful tips. I received so much more than tips. Mickie was very thorough and hit on all the most popular social media platforms. But, what I wasn't expecting was the one on one web appointment where I could ask questions most pertinent to me. And, even after the class was over I had a few more questions that I emailed her and she responded quickly. I highly recommend Mickie's class, expertise and book."

~Karyn Sarganis Fritz
ksf photography & design
karyn@ksfphotography.com

"Mickie has a wealth of smart ideas for marketing our business! She comes up with great ways to reach customers via partnering. Mickie is clever about making sure we connect with customers who are close and easy to reach, some groups we might have otherwise overlooked."

~Darci Frank
Design by Darci
designbydarci@gmail.com

"Dragonfly Ranch has been instrumental in growing our marketing presence in the catering community. Mickie's expertise has proved extremely beneficial for our business and her passion for helping businesses grow is unmatched. This has been one of, if not the greatest partnership we have experienced as a company."

~Chef Joe Thompson
Crisp Catering & Gold Rush Grille
CrispCatering.com

"Mickie has a true gift for helping others get noticed, both businesses and individuals. Her expertise in social media, marketing, and publicity along with her unique style and desire to help others ensures those she works with get their desired results."

~Deanna Cooper Gillingham RN, CCM
Case Management Institute®
CaseManagementInstitute.com